Thanks for your interest in my book & work. That means so much to me!

[signature] Aug 9/22

FriesenPress

Suite 300 - 990 Fort St
Victoria, BC, V8V 3K2
Canada

www.friesenpress.com

**Copyright © 2020 by Laura Sukorokoff**
First Edition — 2020

All rights reserved.

No part of this publication may be reproduced in any form, or by any means, electronic or mechanical, including photocopying, recording, or any information browsing, storage, or retrieval system, without permission in writing from FriesenPress.

ISBN
978-1-5255-6844-2 (Hardcover)
978-1-5255-6845-9 (Paperback)
978-1-5255-6846-6 (eBook)

1. BUSINESS & ECONOMICS, HUMAN RESOURCES & PERSONNEL MANAGEMENT

Distributed to the trade by The Ingram Book Company

# IT'S NOT THEM, IT'S YOU

## Why Employees "Break Up" With Their Managers and What To Do About It

### LAURA SUKOROKOFF

# ADVANCE PRAISE FOR
## IT'S NOT THEM, IT'S YOU

*"In IT'S NOT THEM, IT'S YOU, Laura Sukorokoff masterfully delivers that rarest of books with cover-to-cover stories, lessons, and a framework that brings back the lost art of respect. A must-read, but only if you want to improve relations with your team."*

—Dan Pontefract, best-selling author of OPEN TO THINK and FLAT ARMY

*"Managers have a major impact on employee engagement and retention. Whether you're navigating your first management role or you're a seasoned performer, the advice and tools offered by experienced corporate trainer, Laura Sukorokoff in her candid new book, IT'S NOT THEM, IT'S YOU, provide a well-defined roadmap to establishing and maintaining connection to your team and to creating a winning team culture. Using direct, upfront language and real-world stories, Laura identifies the key reasons employees "break up" with their managers, and outlines the straightforward steps and processes required to stem the tide of high cost employee turnover. The world has changed but, as Laura expertly points out, purposefully creating and preserving relationships with your team is still the most major influence on engagement and why someone chooses to stay or go. People crave feedback, conversations, connection, respect and empowerment from their managers and team leaders. Kudos to Laura for outlining a successful approach to management that does what it's supposed to do - support and retain highly engaged employees."*

—Glorie Averbach, CEO of myCEO

*"Everyone knows great managers retain, engage and even inspire their people... and Laura's book provides concrete, practical ways to achieve this kind of leadership."*

—Bart Egnal, President and CEO of The Humphrey Group

This book is dedicated to Robin and Natasha, who believed in me every step of the way and, in-so-doing, encouraged me to believe in myself and undertake this adventure.

For that, I will always be grateful. ♡

# Table of Contents

**WHY DID I WRITE THIS BOOK?** ................................................... XIII

**PART 1: THE STORIES** ............................................................. 1

    Let's Start with the Stories ................................................. 1

    Rosalie ........................................................................ 4

    Emily ......................................................................... 10

    Simone ....................................................................... 17

    Percy ......................................................................... 23

    Elton ......................................................................... 28

    Caitlin ........................................................................ 33

    Tom .......................................................................... 39

**PART 2: THE OVERARCHING THEME** ........................................... 47

    The Overarching Theme ..................................................... 47

**PART 3: WHAT TO DO** ............................................................ 51

    What You Can Do About It .................................................. 51

    Relationships ................................................................ 52

    Empathy ..................................................................... 69

    Support ...................................................................... 78

    Promotion ................................................................... 88

    Empowerment ............................................................... 94

    Consideration ............................................................... 101

    Trust ......................................................................... 108

**RESPECT ME** ...................................................................... 119

**WRAPPING IT ALL UP** ...................................................... 125

**ACKNOWLEDGEMENTS AND GRATITUDE** ....................... 133

**SOURCES** ........................................................................... 135

**ABOUT THE AUTHOR** ....................................................... 141

Dear Manager,

It's not me ... it's you.

Things used to be so good. I loved seeing you every day at our usual meeting places, and really enjoyed our conversations about how well things were going. It seemed like we had such a bright future ahead of us.

But then things changed. We didn't talk anymore, and I had no idea where this relationship was going. Although you told me you cared, it felt like you didn't really understand me and what I was going through. And when I needed support, you weren't there for me.

This was not an easy decision to come to, but I think it's time I move on. I have options, you know, and I will find someone who appreciates me for who I am.

I wish you luck and hope you'll come to realize the error of your ways. Please learn from this and use your newfound knowledge to make your next relationship better.

Signed,

*Your former employee*

# Why Did I Write This Book?

While writing this book, I've met all kinds of people—each with a story to share. No matter where I am when I talk about my book, I find people want to tell me about their experiences, good and bad.

Like many writers, I do some of my best work in coffee shops (thank you to all the Starbucks and Waves locations that have made this possible). While there, I find I'm often engaged in conversation. Take, for instance, the two women I met one Saturday afternoon. They started conversing with me, asking what I was working on. When I told them it was a book, they immediately asked what it was about. And when I told them what it was about, they both had stories to share.

It's clear this topic resonates with many of us.

Let me start by making something clear—I am not a therapist, nor am I an academic. I didn't undertake a study or craft a research paper based on years of scientific research. What I am is a learning and development professional, coach, and mentor. In those roles, I have people looking to me for knowledge, experience, skill upgrading, and, yes, a sympathetic ear. My work involves developing relationships with people. In so doing, I learn a great deal about the people I'm with. They look to me to guide them through rough patches, to help them with what to say and how to say it, and to provide insight into making things better. Over time, the people I work with come to trust me. That feeling of being able to trust in someone gives them the courage to open up and be vulnerable. I am truly privileged to be the one entrusted with their hopes and fears, and I find myself drawn into their situations, wanting to help.

Over the last couple of years, I began noticing a theme behind these stories. Each of the people I've spoken to had started a job with the best possible intentions. They poured themselves into their work and loved what they did. The operative word here is "loved"—past tense. After a while in the job (the amount of time in the job varied, but in most cases, it was less than two years), things took a bad turn and they ceased to enjoy their work. These employees couldn't wait to get out and find something else that had to be better. Digging further, I found the common thread was the relationship they had with their managers. These toxic relationships were enough to make them miserable and preoccupied them to the extent they were no longer doing their best work. Some dreaded going into the office. Others were bored and simply putting in time, collecting a paycheck until something better came along. Still others fought for their jobs and hoped against hope for change, which never came. The cause of this malaise, in every case, was their relationship—or lack thereof—with their managers.

Many of us have experienced managers behaving badly, and it's reassuring to know that others have had bad experiences as well. After all, misery loves company. I believe that's why so many people have willingly shared their stories with me. More than that, though, I believe they've shared their stories because they think (as I do) that things don't have to end up this way. This book may help to change that. I've chosen seven stories for this book, but I have a lineup of people offering material for future books. That, in and of itself, says something about the business environment out there.

All of the examples in this book are taken from the North American business community. However, that doesn't mean the feelings and experiences of disengagement are isolated to that part of the world. Research shows us that, throughout the world, much of the workforce is disengaged. Recently, I traveled to Africa. I met a man in Nairobi and, as so often happens, our conversation turned to this book. When he learned what it was about, he was excited. He told me there are a great many managers in the African business community who could learn from me, and he hopes my book finds its way to that continent.

This book highlights the stories of seven people who have had bad (sometimes very bad) experiences with their managers. The people come from a variety of backgrounds and workplaces, but managers behaving badly is their common experience. The perspectives shared in the book are told, purposely, from the employee's perspective. I haven't reached out to the managers involved for a few reasons:

- Some of the people who have entrusted me with their stories have done so because I promised them anonymity. If I had spoken to their former managers, I would have broken that trust.

- Managers may very well feel justified in behaving as they do. In so doing, however, they neglect an understanding of how their actions affect others. The lessons contained in this book are born from an appreciation for the effect a manager's bad behaviour has on the people who report to them.

- I've learned that most managers in the business world do not have the kind of relationship with their people that enables them to understand where their team members are coming from, how they work, and what they need to do their best work. This book presents the cause of employee dissatisfaction and the effect of it on their productivity, engagement, and retention so that managers can gain an understanding of what their people need to be successful.

A great many managers feel they need be aggressive, hard, bossy, and otherwise difficult in order to gain respect. I've learned this behaviour tends to have the opposite effect, and the research presented in this book supports this theory. As you go through the book, you'll read real stories of real people, working with real managers in real companies. I haven't named any names, but I am certain the situations presented will be familiar to most readers. The stories themselves tend to deal with the "soft skills" or the Emotional Quotient (EQ) aspects of management, and the research presented backs it up with hard data. I also have drawn from my own personal experiences. I've had some good managers and some bad managers in my long career. Guess which ones I stayed with the longest.

If you are an experienced manager, and you recognize some of your behaviour when you read these stories, I hope you'll gain the knowledge you need to take a new approach with your team members. One of the people who shared their story asked why I was writing this book, since the manager in question would probably never read it. Fair enough. After all, this manager probably thinks his way of working with his direct reports is already very effective. Bosses like that seldom realize the actual effect they're having on their team members. However, since there's an outside chance they will read this book, my hope is that they'll recognize themselves in these pages and learn from what I have to share.

If you are an aspiring manager, I hope you'll learn you don't have to take that aggressive, hard-line approach to be effective in managing the people who report to you. The seven leadership topics presented, along with the overarching theme of the book, are what you need to gain trust, loyalty, buy-in, and productivity from your team members.

# Part 1: The Stories

## LET'S START WITH THE STORIES

When people start a new job, they are fully engaged, excited about the new opportunity, and want to do great work and make a positive impression. Most of them are looking forward to a career with the company and future developmental opportunities the job will bring. They've brought their knowledge, skills, and abilities to the new role and they genuinely want to do good work.

Those who have found passion in their work are so engaged and excited about what they do, they are able to create excitement in others. They get involved in social committees, organizing events, often being the first ones to sign up for them. They are the first to arrive in the morning and are frequently the most productive members on the team. Not only do they pour themselves into their jobs, but they ask for more challenges, volunteer for more projects, and support their team members unflaggingly. They are also the people who bring others to the organization—not for the referral bonus (although they do appreciate that), but because they honestly feel their company is a great place for their friends to work.

In other words, they are highly engaged in their jobs—and are dream employees.

According to Tim Rutledge, author of *Getting Engaged: The New Workplace Loyalty*, truly engaged employees are attracted to and inspired by their work ("I want to do this"), committed ("I am dedicated to the success of what I am doing"), and fascinated ("I love what I am doing"). Employees who are highly engaged care deeply about putting in the effort to make their organizations successful.

In this book, we'll look at cases of highly engaged employees who, over time, became so disillusioned with their companies that they felt they had to leave. How does this happen? And why don't managers notice or care to look at the root cause of departures? That's what we're going to explore. As I mentioned previously, although the stories are true, the names of the people involved have been changed. I've also declined to include company names. But here's the thing—the company name doesn't matter, because the types of things that happened in these companies happen in companies all over the world. They aren't unique. And that somehow makes it even worse.

In North America at the time of writing, unemployment rates are historically low. In fact, there is a "talent war" for many roles, and good employees are in demand. Add to that the cost of turnover (recruiting, hiring, and getting replacement employees up to speed is very costly), and it makes good business sense to do what you can to retain productive workers.

It makes sense, yet the current business climate is facing a crisis of employee disengagement.

- 15% of employees worldwide are fully engaged.[1]

- 52% of US workers plan to look for a new job and of those who will take part in the hunt, 54% landed their current job less than a year ago.[2]

- Greater than 80% of workers are either actively looking for a new job or are open to one.[3]

- Nearly half of employees said they've quit a job because of a bad manager, 56% think managers are promoted prematurely, and 60% think managers need managerial training.[4]

There are plenty more eyebrow-raising statistics I could present (and some of them are dispersed throughout the book), but I think you get the point.

People are not happy at work and want a new job. The chief cause of this unhappiness is bad managers.

In the next section, the seven featured stories will provide examples of bad management. After looking at these examples, I'll present solutions to change things for the better. It's worth mentioning the solutions are not fancy, in-depth or costly. Rather, they are practical, easy to implement, and something managers can do *right now* to make things better.

# ROSALIE

Rosalie was excited to start her new job. She had been working part-time and contracts for years, while her children were growing up. With the children grown, she was ready to take on the challenge of full-time work and was relishing the opportunity. She quickly landed a job, in a role she was excited about, and she couldn't wait to start.

Rosalie was hired as a business coach for the regional office of a large manufacturing organization. This company used the Net Promoter System (NPS) to measure customer loyalty, and it was experiencing some pretty low scores. Rosalie's goal was simple—raise the NPS from the Detractor score it currently received to Promoter.

Although the goal was simple, this was not an easy job. Rosalie faced many obstacles, including employees who were entrenched in what they had always been doing, who hated the Net Promoter System, and who really didn't see a need to change. Despite that, she dug in and embraced the challenge. Initially, she came up with competitions and activities to engage the team, she pointed out where they were great, and where they were lacking, and coached them all, which resulted in a big upsurge in the NPS score. Within six months, Rosalie was offered a promotion.

Rosalie was a highly engaged employee who worked hard, turned out excellent quality work, and exceeded everyone's expectations. She was often seen calling her husband toward the end of the day to explain she was going to work late, because she was so engrossed in what she was working on. Rosalie loved her work, but she also enjoyed those she worked with. She made friendships and brought in new people to the organization who, in turn, followed her example and put forward their best efforts.

# IT'S NOT THEM, IT'S YOU

Rosalie was inspired to deliver top-notch work because of the actions of her boss who put forward challenging ideas and trusted her to rise to those challenges. In addition, her boss encouraged Rosalie to contribute her own ideas, and to challenge what she put forward. Rosalie immediately produced results, which led to her promotion. She also quickly became one of the most trusted people in the organization (according to Employee Engagement Survey results).

How is it that within a year after getting her promotion, Rosalie was found at her desk, unmotivated, and looking for another job?

Simply knowing Rosalie was looking for work while at work should be enough to tell you she was somewhat disengaged, if not completely disengaged.

## So, what happened?

Shortly after getting her promotion, Rosalie became caught in the middle of a power struggle, because at her company, the leadership team (to whom she reported) was ousted and the old guard took over the company and reclaimed the power. Unfortunately, according to the old guard, the work Rosalie did was viewed as unnecessary and, frankly, as a nuisance. The old attitude of not needing to change crept back in, and Rosalie was nearly back where she started because her work was no longer valued.

Rosalie's new boss questioned her loyalty—outright. She was called into her manager's office and was asked point-blank where her loyalty lay. This was a shock to Rosalie, who was simply doing her job according to stated goals in the best way she could. There was no reason to question her loyalty at all. After being questioned, things started happening that also left Rosalie feeling confused and concerned. Rosalie was working on a large project and was asked to present her work to her boss. After viewing only part of the presentation, her boss asked if it was a joke. This hurt Rosalie, who honestly tried to put something creative and attention-getting into the project. To have it dismissed in such a juvenile and unprofessional manner was hurtful and disrespectful. Rosalie was a high-potential employee who cared greatly about the quality of work she produced and the impact it had on the company. It wasn't that the project missed the mark—Rosalie could deal with that. Rather, it was the spiteful way it was judged that hurt. The feedback she received was not constructive, it was critical. And more than a little insulting and humiliating. With the old guard in charge, any attempts at creativity were at best discouraged and at worst mocked.

Throughout the time she spent on the team, Rosalie's boss had a standing weekly one on one scheduled with her. This went well for a few weeks, and then it got shaky. Rosalie noticed the frequency of her one on ones was reduced gradually month over month. She would go to her boss's office for the regular meeting, only to find her boss on the phone or, worse yet, in a meeting with someone else. Rosalie's efforts to reschedule the meetings were typically ignored. Compounding this was the fact that often Rosalie would go to her boss's office for their meeting, only to find she was away on business or vacation, even though not a word about her schedule changes had been mentioned to Rosalie.

At this stage it becomes easy to see why Rosalie would be feeling neglected and unmotivated. After all, she went from someone who was highly regarded, had been promoted, and was very involved in projects while collaborating with her old boss, to someone who wasn't valued or respected enough to be informed that meetings were cancelled.

Furthermore, Rosalie learned that most days her boss would go and greet all the members of her team that were near her office. Her desk was in a different corner of the building, and she rarely received the same treatment. Sometimes she would wander around, sharing a story and a laugh with each of her team members, but she was seldom involved in team meetings, often left out of communications, and otherwise ignored.

Is it any wonder Rosalie wanted another job?

## What did she wish would have happened?

Rosalie's needs were quite simple. What she wanted was a boss who would respect her as an employee, value her contributions, and who wanted to develop a relationship with her. She wished the boss would honour the meeting commitments and treat her as a valued member of her team.

Rosalie would have appreciated some recognition for her efforts. In addition, she would have appreciated regular one on one meetings so she could feel in the loop—or at least not feel forgotten in her little corner. As a knowledgeable, previously revered employee and experienced professional, as well as a grown-up, Rosalie deserved that, at the least.

How much effort would it have taken her boss to rectify the situation? Not much, actually. All Rosalie really wanted was for their one on ones to be honoured. If they needed to change, then reschedule. It was the lack of communication that rankled her. In time, that lack of commitment and communication led Rosalie to feel neglected and unwanted.

The other thing Rosalie would have valued was honest and respectful feedback. No one hits the mark continuously, and Rosalie certainly never expected to hit a home run every time. It was the way the feedback was delivered that made the difference to her. By becoming angry and abusive, Rosalie's boss made her feel belittled and like a talentless hack. It's highly likely this wasn't the intention, but unfortunately, it was the result.

Finally, had Rosalie's boss taken the time to get to know her, she would have discovered Rosalie was a dedicated, smart, talented employee who always worked hard to deliver something of quality that would benefit the company and the employees. By not having trust or developing any relationship whatsoever with Rosalie, the boss missed out on creating the kind of synergy that happens when talented people work hard to achieve excellent results.

## What is a manager to do?

The lesson here is pretty straight forward—managers must pay attention to those who report to them. They should put focus on developing relationships with them and respect their time, effort, and feelings.

One on ones, especially when done regularly and with open communication, provide an excellent opportunity to connect with employees. By allowing time for employee concerns, manager concerns, and a review of plans moving forward, both parties are kept in the loop.

Further, one on ones afford an excellent opportunity to develop relationships. By spending time together, both manager and employee learn what makes the other tick. Issues that affect the employee, the team, the department, and the company can be discussed, and the employee will know how her or his efforts contribute to overall success.

When time is invested in developing the relationship, managers also have the opportunity to develop trust. Remember, trust is something earned—not automatically given to someone just because they're the boss. If managers want their reports to trust them and they want to be able to trust their reports, they need to invest time developing relationships.

In this way, one can learn how to best provide constructive feedback that will be well received. It's rare that an employee doesn't care about the quality of their work, so it's a safe bet feedback will be listened to and acted upon. In actual fact, employees want to know where they could improve. The way the message is delivered is as important as the message itself, so it's imperative for managers to remember that no one should be ridiculed. Employees do, however, appreciate the opportunity to get back on track and perform their best.

## Lessons learned

- Managers should schedule one on ones. Ideally these should take place weekly, but even bi-weekly would be sufficient. Managers often say they don't have the time for one on ones and coaching. I'm arguing they don't have the time NOT to do this. Ultimately, managers will have more time available because they can trust their reports to carry out the work that needs to be done.

- Managers should honour their commitment to regular one on one meetings. Employees want to feel important and valued. By keeping commitments (or not) managers demonstrate just how important (or not) the development of the employee is to them.

- Managers should meet with their people, share ideas with them, and help them feel part of the team. Employees know when they're being ignored. One might think they would enjoy being out of the manager's line of sight, but this isn't the case.

- Managers should be open and approachable with team members; they will appreciate it.

- Managers should build relationships that create trust, open dialogue and have full transparency.[1] That's what great managers do.

# EMILY

Emily began work with a large company as a business coach. She was ideally suited to the position, since she had a firm grasp of business strategy, and a warm and nurturing personality that encouraged people and led them to trust her. She genuinely liked the people she worked with, and they liked her. Emily had many friends in the office, and she was a fixture in company events. She was quick to laugh, and people felt she was truly an advocate for them when she coached them.

Emily coached frontline staff on how to better serve their customers. She understood that engaged, happy employees created a better experience for customers, which ultimately led to higher customer satisfaction and more sales. Her efforts led to a rise in service metrics that was noticeable throughout the company.

Emily thrived in her role and did amazing work. She had a boss who supported her, and in return, Emily put forward her best efforts all the time. In addition, Emily had coworkers who made the day fun and with whom she developed friendships outside the office.

Then things started to change. Her boss went on maternity leave, so Emily had to report to someone else, who started seeing a new direction for her work. Not long after, one of Emily's closest friends at the office was downsized out of the company, closely followed by a second friend. With two colleagues gone, her area of the workspace became quiet. And then, there was a change in senior leadership, which meant a new strategic direction for many departments.

Emily was put into a new role. She was no longer a business coach, but she did train and support other employees, coaching them on new processes and procedures. Again, this was well in her wheelhouse, and she embraced the new role, pouring herself into her work. She put in overtime and happily travelled when asked to. Although some of her friends were gone, Emily knew she was doing meaningful work, and she stayed on with the company and her new team. There were moments when she felt comfortable and part of the team, but then something changed.

She began to feel like an outsider on her own team. When Emily's manager, who worked remotely, came to town, he would frequently come into the office and not even acknowledge her with a "hi" or "how are you". Most of the time, she wouldn't even know he was in town, and he didn't take the opportunity to schedule one on ones. She felt that her manager was always a bit removed and too busy for her. He wouldn't even make time to help Emily out with questions. As a coach and problem solver, she figured that it was up to her to find solutions. Emily knew something about herself—if she was asking a question, it was because she'd already exhausted other avenues and she really needed help finding a solution. So, by turning her away and asking Emily to find her own solutions, her manager was delaying the progress of work, and in the process, making Emily feel like a bother.

Then, Emily had an accident that left her in excruciating pain. It didn't occur at work, so, to be fair to the company, they had no line of sight into the severity of the injury or the prognosis. They had to trust Emily's word and communications from the doctor. Emily asked for one month off, unpaid, to recover. The response from the company was that two weeks should be sufficient. It seemed as if they felt they knew better than Emily and her doctors what was good for her.

Emily spent the next year in pain. Even so, she steadfastly worked through it, not dropping any balls at work. This came at a high personal cost. Her recovery process was delayed because she wasn't allowed adequate rest in the beginning stages. Eventually Emily realized that she had to take more time to recover and if she didn't, her long-term health and ability to work would be at risk. When she advised her boss of her need to take time off, she received no acknowledgement. The same dismissive attitude applied to her coworkers when she reached out about assigned tasks. Again, Emily felt like an outsider, but this time it was worse. She was feeling ignored. When communication did occur, there was scant acknowledgement of the physical challenges she was facing. The team was just looking for work to be done. To Emily, it seemed like they were angry with her for her medical problems.

Emily was moved to another team, reporting to a new boss. This boss seemed much more sympathetic to what Emily was going through and was more supportive. There were times when she was called upon to come in for meetings or to travel for projects, but her efforts to work through the pain were sincerely appreciated by this new boss.

In spite of the supportive relationship Emily had with her new boss, she faced more roadblocks with the company. She needed special ergonomic equipment, and felt like a burden when she approached Human Resources for help. She received compassionate responses from some people, and nothing from others. So, she worked with her insurance company to get the equipment she needed to allow her to work at the office. No one from the company was willing to work with her on finding her way; she was left to fend for herself.

Eventually, Emily made the decision to quit the company. The pain she was experiencing and the pressure to work through it meant that Emily's personal life was suffering. She felt shut down when she was at her most vulnerable. Although she felt bad about leaving her new manager, she knew she couldn't work for a company that didn't support people when they really needed it.

## So, what happened?

This story is a little different from the others in that it isn't just about the actions of any one manager. It was the company that let Emily down. However, there are still lessons in this scenario for managers.

After putting in so many years of great work with the company, Emily (rightly) expected they would trust that she was telling the truth about her injury and understand why she couldn't return to work as before. Outwardly, Emily didn't display casts or crutches, but the pain and injury were real nonetheless. The fact the company, and her previous manager, didn't seem to believe she was really in pain hurt her emotionally. She felt shut down when she was already in a vulnerable state.

Had she felt supported in her recovery and with help finding solutions to address her physical limitations, or even an interest from her team in working with her, Emily may have simply taken a medical leave. If Emily's second manager had had regular one on ones with her, they may have developed the kind of relationship where he was willing to listen and understand what she was going through, and she would have felt supported and loyal to the company. Instead, she felt alone and wondered why she was working for a company that didn't support her.

Emily had three bosses in just a few years, and really didn't have the opportunity to develop a deep relationship with any of them. The last of her managers was definitely the most involved, but even he didn't really understand what she was going through. In addition, he didn't advocate on her behalf. At a time when Emily could have used an ally, he took a back seat, leaving her to fight her battles. It's no wonder she felt alone.

After a time, Emily wondered why she would even want to stay with a company that treated her that way. Eventually it came to a point where she asked herself, "Why am I putting myself in a situation where I am suffering?"

## What did she wish would have happened?

Emily felt bad about the whole situation. She felt she was letting down her manager and the company when she had no control over her circumstances. All she really wanted was for her manager and team members to believe in her and to understand that she really was injured, not shirking work.

Emily would have appreciated not feeling like a burden. Perhaps she felt this way because she never really felt connected to her team. The manager she had for most of her tenure with the company was distant. He worked remotely and frequently ignored her when he was in the office. Emily is a warm and friendly person, and he likely would have enjoyed getting to know her, just as her next (and last manager at the company) did. That manager appreciated the work she did and made time for her. Sadly, it wasn't enough. The manager she had for the longest time should have done the same thing—appreciate her work and make time for her.

With regard to her injury, Emily feels the company could have done a lot more to support her recovery and accommodate her requests for special equipment to mitigate her physical pain while she was at the office. The stress that arose out of having to work through her pain, explain herself over and over, and fight for any equipment and concessions was too much. It would have been nice had the people in Human Resources—who are supposed to be responsible for helping employees work through these situations—taken an interest in helping her, or even displayed some empathy. Again, her manager would have been a welcome ally, had it been considered.

## What is a manager to do?

As mentioned above, it was the actions of the company on the whole that prompted Emily to leave. But all three managers were certainly involved and each bear some responsibility.

Management 101 speaks to the importance of regular and frequent one on ones with team members in developing strong and effective working relationships. The manager's actions also led the team members to distance themselves from Emily, resulting in her feeling isolated and out of the loop. Not making time for Emily when she needed help (which was the case even before she was injured) meant she needed more time to complete assignments. She couldn't get answers to questions when she needed them, and had to take extra time to do research. It would have been easy to change this. Managers should hold frequent one on ones, encourage team meetings and collaboration, and regularly communicate with team members. Again, Management 101.

If a manager has a good relationship with an employee, they will become familiar with how they work, and know when they need help and support. Showing compassion toward suffering encourages loyalty, good work, and speedier recoveries.

Managers are wise to consider how what they do impacts those who report to them and who follows them. Not only did the manager's behaviour impact Emily, it also impacted those she worked with. Leading with compassion encourages others to feel compassionate, which in turn leads those on their teams to support teammates who are suffering.

This last part should be self-evident. Managers need to remember the golden rule: *Treat others as you would like to be treated.* Treating your team members as humans with physical, emotional, and work needs will help you to relate to them and encourage them to do better work.

## Lessons learned

Empathy is something many managers feel uncomfortable with. Yet it is one of the very best ways to connect with employees.

- Managers should build relationships with their reports. Effective leaders cultivate relationships in order to get to know the people they work with by listening to their frustrations and joys and caring about them.[1]

- Managers should understand they have more influence than they know over the actions of their team members. They guide their people about how to think, feel, and act when suffering presents itself.[2]

- Managers should encourage caring in their teams. By emphasizing a culture of compassion and caring, organizations can expect better results in terms of employee satisfaction and reduced costs from absenteeism, burnout, or turnover.[3]

- Managers should create a culture of inclusion. By excluding team members who are suffering, compassion fades from the picture and team members cease working together and begin working with an "every person for themselves" attitude.

- Managers should realize chronic pain is real. According to the Laser Spine Institute, chronic pain can lead to stress, but stress can also worsen chronic pain. By knowingly or unknowingly creating stressful work situations (like those in which people feel cast out from their teams, untrusted, unsupported, or unappreciated), managers are also causing the recovery period for their employees to be lengthened. The net effect is that they are less productive for a longer time. And that means higher costs for the company.

# SIMONE

Simone worked really hard to get her new job. She completed a written assignment and went through multiple job interviews, including sitting before a panel of executives to land the job. She was excited and felt proud of herself for receiving the offer. After all, she had beaten out several other qualified candidates to land it. In her mind, that said something about what she brought to the table.

She started working with her new team, who all seemed pleased to have her on board. At the onset, Simone felt stimulated by the work she was doing. She loved her team, liked her boss, and liked the work, which led to lots of overtime—and she didn't mind at all. One of Simone's beliefs was that work is a large part of one's life. It's personal, and thus she made friends at the office and that fulfilled her personal life as well.

Simone took satisfaction from the fact she was able, early on, to start digging in and making changes that lightened the load for others she worked with. Small wonder they liked having her there! Her boss was based in another city, but that didn't really bother Simone. He gave her great direction, and she felt as if they collaborated on the best approach for her position. He would ask her in their one on ones what her plans were for the week and what she needed from him to do her work. His attitude was "Let's succeed as a team," so she felt secure in the fact she had access to what she needed to be successful in her work. Although this was her first time taking on a role of this sort— it was a brand-new role in the company—Simone was reassured they were in it together.

And then, a new boss came into the picture (by now you should be picking up on the fact that this is a familiar theme). Simone was sent a message, asking her to go to the office of a senior manager. Once there, the news was delivered that this manager would be her new boss. On top of that, she was informed there was also a change in focus for her role. Once again, she would be moving into uncharted territory. But this time she didn't feel she was supported.

Although she was asked how she felt about reporting to this new boss, Simone didn't feel she could reply honestly. When I asked her how she answered, her reply was, "What could I say?" Simone's previous boss had the "We'll figure it out together" attitude. The new boss had the attitude of, "I'm not here to answer questions. Ask around the company and figure it out yourself." It was clear this new boss didn't want her as a direct report, and that was hard for Simone to understand. Worse yet, he intimidated and bullied her, making fun of her accent and the way she wrote. She felt that everyone else in the company appeared to like her, so where was she going wrong with this guy?

Not long after this transition, Simone—the employee who dug in and did great work, who was not just friendly, but friends with so many in the company, and the employee who was so happy to be working there—was fired. Truth be told, she had already been looking for other work, after less than a year on the job. The thought occurred to her that perhaps the company did her a favour by forcing her to leave.

## So, what happened?

While the position Simone occupied was highly valued by the leader of one team, it was clearly not a strategic advantage for the new manager and his team. Her new boss told her he didn't like having to fit her into his team, but *his* boss had the last word, so he had to go along with it. Because he made it apparent that he didn't want Simone on his team from day one, the new manager intimidated Simone to the point where she stumbled on her words and became flustered in his presence. This added fuel to his fire, and he began to bully her—pushing her to the point where she tried to avoid him as much as possible and worked from home as often as she could.

Simone was used to a team that respected her and valued her work. She was also used to a boss who believed she was adding value and gave her guidance and support when she needed it. To report to someone who didn't respect or like her resulted in Simone feeling intimidated to the point where she lost confidence, stumbled over her words, and questioned her work.

She felt abandoned because there was no stability, no support, and no one to turn to for coaching and guidance. The person who was supposed to lead and coach her clearly didn't want anything to do with her.

## What did she wish would have happened?

The answer to this is probably obvious. It's easy for us to think what she wanted was for her new boss to like her, or at least respect her and not bully her. But that's not actually what she really wished would have happened.

When I asked Simone this question, her reply was that she wished the new boss would have been honest and let his boss know that he didn't want her as a report. Further, she wished his superior would have noticed that her new manager did not get along with her and would have moved Simone to another department. She has no doubt she could have continued to do good work with a different boss, one who appreciated and valued her contributions.

She also wished this manager had taken the time to fully get to know his direct reports so that he understood more about her and what she appreciates in a manager. While she didn't need handholding, she would have benefitted from some direction, guidance, and support.

Finally, she wished the new manager had appreciated the skills she brought to the table. Simone did work she was proud of and which benefitted the company. No worth was applied to that.

## What is a manager to do?

Managers must remember their employees are people, not things or tasks. If they are in a position of leadership, then they should lead. There is no place for bullying or intimidation in a respectful workplace. But even if they are the sort that is tempted to act that way, it must be understood it is *not* the way to encourage people to do their best work.

Managers must support and encourage employees. It's fine to be the type of manager that doesn't want to have to hold an employee's hand. However, they should encourage and support their reports in their efforts to figure out solutions. When employees set out to "figure things out," they're putting themselves at risk of failure. Knowing this, it's understandable they would be tentative about seeking out solutions if they lack a leader who has their back. Simone felt her leader was setting her up for failure, which caused her to feel not only tentative, but downright scared of doing anything less than perfect. Her only support option was to enlist the help of people in other departments who offered their opinions and suggestions. At the end of the day, she had no way to know if that was what her boss actually wanted.

Additionally, the new manager should have examined Simone's track record. She had consistently delivered great work, was highly productive, and had been a trailblazer in a new role that had become integral to the company's processes moving forward. Simone was hired to face a problem and find solutions. She did a good job of it with the support of her old manager, but faced stalls and setbacks with her new boss. Here again, it comes down to support. Managers need to realize their employees may not get things perfect on the first try. So, the role of the manager is to help them identify what went wrong and how to fix it moving forward. They must demonstrate that it's okay to try and fail; to learn and improve is a key factor in supporting employees.

## Lessons learned

- Managers should talk to their people and develop relationships with them. They should learn what drives them and what they need to excel. In addition, managers must keep an open mind, and over time may come to appreciate all their reports—even the ones they weren't so crazy about having on their teams.

- Managers should create a supportive environment. If managers want their people to be creative and bring forth ideas, then they must create a safe and supportive space for them to do so. If managers punish or ridicule their reports when they fail, their reports will understandably be reluctant to take any future risks.

- Managers should look at the work the employee has done in the past to know what they're capable of in the future. If they have recognized problems in the past and had breakthrough ideas to solve them, it's likely they will do that same level of work for any manager, given support and encouragement.

- Managers should learn how to handle frustration, especially if they don't personally like someone on their team. Managers must be honest with themselves about what pushes their buttons and realize employees don't intend to push those buttons. They didn't even know the buttons were installed! If the manager can figure out what triggers him or her, it will be easier to figure out how to deal with it.

- Managers should put on a good front. If managers have reports they can't like, they must at least be fair, impartial, and pay attention to opportunities to appreciate them and the work they deliver. Employees want their managers to like them and acknowledge the work they do. Managers may never come to like particular employees, but they might bring themselves to appreciate their value.

- Managers should seek out the positives. They should look for things their reports do well and attributes they *can* appreciate. There is always something to like about people. In one on ones, managers should look for things they have in common to build on.

- Managers should do their best to be fair and unbiased at review time, even if they don't personally like an employee (maybe *especially* then). They should focus on the work their reports did. Was it good quality work? If so, they deserve appropriate recognition. Managers must be honest with themselves and assess whether they are evaluating each of their reports objectively and on the same basis. If not, then they have to fix that.

- Finally—and this really should go without saying— managers should not bully their team members (or anyone else, for that matter). Bullying and harassment should never exist in the workplace. Managers do not have the right to bully their reports, EVER.

# PERCY

Percy worked as a project manager for a tech company. He loved his job, because it allowed him to get involved in many areas of the company. He reported to the chief operating officer, and did great work for her, because she gave him some juicy projects. The COO championed Percy, bringing him into meetings, speaking about him to other leaders, and basically promoting his interests throughout the organization. In return, Percy worked hard and produced some amazing work. He garnered a reputation as someone that could be relied on in the organization to take hold of a project and efficiently and effectively drive it through to completion.

It's a fact that in every company there are people who are not so happy where they are. Percy could often be seen chatting with these people, advising them on the reasons why they should stay with the company. He mentored other employees, and always had time to help people with their problems and concerns. Percy himself was someone who was seeking different opportunities. He was ambitious, and he very much appreciated how the COO recognized his potential and championed him in the company.

And then it happened. The COO left the company and Percy was assigned to another executive. Immediately, he found that getting access to this new manager was next to impossible. Percy had the distinct impression this was because of his reporting relationship with the previous COO. Percy keenly felt that he wasn't a priority at all to his new boss, and that any work to improve the relationship was on Percy to carry out. Not long after the reporting change, Percy was moved to another department, and found himself reporting to another executive, who gave Percy the impression he had no idea what to do with him. Percy got frustrated, because after several months, there was still not much for him to do and no better roles (although promised) were coming through. Percy provided suggestions for new projects and highlighted the work he was capable of doing, but was consistently shut down. Eventually his new boss (his third one) took him to meet with a senior manager, telling Percy he would now be reporting to her. This was a shock to Percy. Not only had he not seen it coming, but no one explained to him why it was happening.

The COO's departure early on in Percy's tenure at the company was significant. She had been a champion for him and was always working to promote Percy's interests. Percy felt motivated and challenged by her—as if there was a true sense of accomplishment and progression. Under the others, he felt as if his career was being stalled, because he was not given the opportunity to perform. Under his first boss, Percy had been enthusiastic about the company. He was a cheerleader, and his passionate beliefs in his projects encouraged others to want to be involved. For example, after the launch of one of his projects, Percy had multiple employees volunteering to be part of the team. This passion quickly died as his new leaders just didn't know what to do with him. Promised promotions didn't come through, and even an annual raise didn't materialize for him. He was advised at wage increase time that he already made a very good salary, so the budget for raises was spent on others.

I'm sure you can imagine how Percy felt. He had the distinct impression that no one knew what to do with him. About eighteen months earlier, Percy had been on a fast track to a leadership role. He had an executive sponsor who was promoting his capabilities and interests across the organization. Now he had a boss that didn't know why he was reporting to her. Percy felt he had no control over his situation and had no way to tackle his concerns head-on. He knew his original boss had his back, and thought his third boss had his back too, so he felt betrayed when he was shuffled unceremoniously to a new department, reporting to a lower-level manager and was passed over for raises and promotions. By this point, he felt angry and was ready to move on to another company that would help him achieve his career goals. When asked if he would have stayed if a leadership role became open, Percy replied, "Maybe." However, at that point, he was so ready to move on, he might not have even taken the opportunity that had been his goal all along.

## So, what happened?

It was clear the various teams Percy was placed with had not factored a role like Percy's into their strategic plan—and their efforts to do so were limited. Percy's role as a project manager continued, but he was no longer involved in the planning meetings, so he had limited knowledge as to what was going on. He had to put together pieces of information he gleaned from his manager and apply his best interpretation. What made things worse was that Percy had limited visibility, but full accountability, if things went wrong. And even though his managers knew of his role within their teams, they were never prepared for what would happen when Percy finished a project and no plan for what Percy would work on next.

After the COO left, Percy felt there was no longer anyone within the company to champion him. He had the distinct impression that the person who stepped into the COO's role didn't like him because of his previous relationship with the former COO. Any efforts to communicate with his new boss left Percy feeling frustrated and shut out. This feeling carried on with the next two bosses—they all left him feeling unimportant and insignificant.

After several months, Percy was convinced there was no future with the organization. So, he left.

## What did he wish would have happened?

Percy, like most employees, is motivated by a sense of progression, of moving forward in their careers. By constantly being stalled in his forward progression without being given reasons, Percy lost his desire to put forward his best efforts. Further, he lost his attachment to the company and his desire to mentor others. He firmly felt that he needed to work for someone who recognized potential and valued the work output and the knowledge, experience, and skills employees bring with them.

Percy would have appreciated a transparent conversation with his leaders, informing him of a potential career path and providing him with the sense of forward momentum he craved. He wished that the new managers had taken an interest in him enough to know that upward momentum motivated him, and the lack of it is what ultimately drove him out the door. Furthermore, Percy would have flourished had his work been recognized and rewarded with an annual raise. It felt unfair that others received this benefit, and he was passed over.

In all cases, what Percy missed was the "why" behind the decisions made for him and about him. He felt he had much more to give the company and couldn't understand why he was stymied in his efforts.

## What is a manager to do?

Managers must talk to their employees and find out what truly motivates them. If the employee is like Percy, they should listen to what they say and work with them to create a career path they will find challenging and motivating. In their one on one conversations, they should ask them where they would like to go in the company and create a plan for the best way to get there. This is important! Managers must support their employee's efforts to get there. This includes recognizing their efforts and granting them bonuses and raises that are commensurate with the work they have done. If a manager doesn't feel an employee's assessment of their progress lines up with the manager's assessment, then they should share why. It's important they convey exactly why the rewards allocated don't line up with their expectations.

Additionally, with a role that requires understanding the strategic direction of the company and how projects fit in with the strategy, managers must be sure to include those people in meetings and communications that will affect them. It's a demotivating force to remove people from these communications when they used to be part of them. If they must be removed, then the team member deserves an explanation of why and how they will be provided with information they need for the project going forward.

## Lessons learned

In a tight labour market, like the one North America is currently experiencing, companies can't afford to have people leaving left and right. Retention should be a top priority.

- Managers should ensure their employees are very satisfied with their current jobs. According to LinkedIn, only 15% say they **wouldn't** move if a better opportunity comes along. (Source: https://www.inc.com/laura-montini/infographic/inside-the-hearts-and-minds-of-professionals-everywhere.html)

- Managers should understand opportunities for advancement is in the top three motivators for employees. So are better compensation and benefits. By denying Percy of these, his managers opened the door to him going elsewhere.

- Managers should understand their employees' career goals, and act as an advocate for them within the company. They shouldn't just shuffle them to another department, leaving the distinct impression they're no longer wanted. Instead, they should share why the decision was made to move them, and what benefits they will receive as a result of this career move.

- Managers should familiarize themselves with the research. According to Mercer's 2018 Global Talent Trends Study:

  - Employees must grow, change, and thrive. If they don't get it from their company, they'll look for it elsewhere.

  - Managers should reward employees in exchange for their individual efforts if they want them to thrive.

  - Managers must leverage and unleash the potential of employees through a "human touch."

- Managers should ask themselves what they are doing to encourage their people to stay with the company and to grow within it. If the answer is nothing, again, they're opening the door for them to go.

# ELTON

Elton worked for his company for over three years, enjoying every aspect of his job. The travel and networking involved fed into his love for exploring new cultures. He combined his desire for adventure with a career he found fulfilling and exciting.

Then one day, it came crashing to a halt. There was a new VP in town, and that shook up everything.

Elton's previous boss was well loved by the team. He allowed people to shine, and gave them credit for their good work. As a result, they were fiercely loyal to him and trusted him to lead them anywhere. Elton was no different—he enjoyed an open and transparent working relationship with his boss and appreciated how he was trusted to do great work.

Enter the new boss. This man had little to no experience in the industry. Even so, he started his tenure in the role by criticizing the old management and the way the department had been run. Further, he made sure they knew he was there to clean up the mess. The thing is, Elton and his teammates didn't think things actually were a mess. They considered themselves a high-performing team, and the company had always viewed them as such. However, this new manager was shaking everything up and telling them that what they had carefully constructed over the years was amateur and needed to be rebuilt.

The new boss wasted no time cleaning house and reworking the team. He let some key members go and shuffled others around. Some people were elevated, while others were left wondering what they'd done wrong.

Probably the worst of it was the way the new boss criticized the work of the old boss. Elton felt he was constantly in the position of defending his old boss, his teammates, and the work they had done. This resulted in the new boss questioning Elton's loyalty and placing him under a microscope.

Elton wasn't used to this, and chafed under the scrutiny. He felt that he had earned the trust of his previous boss and had done nothing to jeopardize that, so why then did he feel his opinions were not just unwelcome, but also irrelevant? Why was he asked to justify his every move? In the past, Elton had been given the latitude to exercise his best judgment. Now, he was required to run every little thing past his manager.

After more than three years on the job, Elton would still have described himself as highly engaged with every department in the company, and on great terms with his customers. He received enthusiastic and positive praise from his customers, but in retrospect, believes that is one of the things that led to his demise (could it be the new boss was jealous of these relationships and wanted them for himself?). Shortly after the new boss took over, Elton was asked to change departments. He was no longer wanted on that team. Instead of taking the offer of the other role, Elton chose to leave the company.

## So, what happened?

Why is a self-proclaimed, highly engaged employee happier to leave the company than take on a different role?

Elton felt as if he were thrown under the bus and was the scapegoat for the "mess" his new manager inherited. He didn't appreciate the way his former boss and teammates were spoken about and so easily dismissed. He didn't want to work in any environment that would allow that to happen. Elton felt he had previously been in a high-functioning team that had been manipulated and transformed so that team members no longer enjoyed the same comradery or worked well together. Instead there was an atmosphere of "every person for themselves."

Elton felt angry, like he had been stabbed in the back. Although he still spoke well of the company (after all, Elton is a true professional), he no longer believed in an organization that tolerated this type of behaviour in one of its teams. He preferred to take a chance on unemployment rather than compromise his ideals.

Elton also felt his hands had been tied. He had not been allowed to communicate with external business contacts (without running things past his boss first) or make decisions about his workflow. There seemed to be no real reason for his manager to exercise this control over Elton, and no reason was ever communicated.

## What did he wish would have happened?

Elton had worked hard to develop relationships with his business contacts. Therefore, it was strange to him that his new manager would have an issue with Elton working directly with them. Instead of viewing what Elton was working on with suspicion, the manager would have been better served to empower Elton to nurture the relationships and continue to grow the business.

Elton would have appreciated his new boss coming in with an open mind and some respect for the legacy he'd inherited, as well as the company, team, and other departments. There had been good work done by the team previously, and as a loyal cheerleader, Elton defended it. Had his new boss come into the team with praise and acknowledgement for what they'd accomplished to date and then encouraged them to explore new ways of thinking, Elton would have made a different choice.

Further, Elton would have liked his new boss to communicate with his team members and not to interpret disagreement as disrespect or disloyalty. Conflict can be good and differing points of view can lead to breakthroughs.

Finally, Elton would have liked his new boss to trust that Elton knew what he was doing and let him keep doing it. He would have appreciated his boss working with him to set goals and objectives, and he would have appreciated feedback and follow-up. After all, his people were *people*, not minions. Instead of micromanagement and suspicion, Elton wanted his new boss to have open, frank, and transparent conversations about what was happening in the company and the department. Elton was eager to share the good work he had done, but found his boss viewed it skeptically and even with jealousy.

## What is a manager to do?

Managers—whether they're new to the company/department or not—must understand the importance of communication. By sharing ideas and collaborating with coworkers, people can come up with amazing, forward-thinking solutions that lead to improved results. And when that happens—when the team looks good—the manager looks great!

Having a strategy and vision for the team and communicating it to them goes a long way in helping decipher priorities and accomplish goals that are aligned with company objectives. That transparency is important to building trust and ensuring team members feel involved and valued.

Empowering employees encourages them to stretch, grow, and do great work. It also frees up the manager to focus on more of the strategic work most managers always wish they had more time for. Managers need to remember that the people who work for them are there for a reason. They have skills, knowledge, abilities, and talents that can be put to work. Why not let them do it?

## Lessons learned

- Managers should communicate frequently. Weekly one on ones would have afforded Elton and his boss the opportunity to develop an effective working relationship. In discussions of this kind, managers can learn a lot about the people they work with. Initial meetings can centre around working style, and later meetings should focus on what's happening with the employee, with the manager, and with the company, leading to an understanding of how to best approach the job and achieve full productivity.

- Managers should communicate consistently. Regular communication would also have helped the manager understand that while Elton was opinionated about his work, his opinions were in the best interest of the company. Elton was a loyal employee, who constantly highlighted what was great about the company to customers. In this case, there was a major opportunity for the manager to gain insight into customer needs, to use those insights to develop products, policies, and procedures, and develop his own profile with the customers over time.

- Managers should trust employees to do their best work, make good decisions, and choose what works for them. It may not be done exactly as the manager would do it, but different styles can still work effectively. Empowering employees to do good work their own way will lead to them feeling strong, capable, and engaged.

- Managers should be transparent with employees. Allowing them into the inner circle (wherever possible) can lead to greater loyalty and engagement. Employees will feel they are part of the process and will put forward their best efforts to make things successful if they understand what's behind it.

- Managers should be aware that disagreement doesn't mean disrespect or mutiny. Much can be gained from considering dissenting points of view. It's from these moments that great ideas can arise. Conflict is simply another form of feedback and communication. Remember, diamonds are formed under pressure. Managers should let their teams work through some friction, because the payoff can be well worth it.

# CAITLIN

Caitlin started working for a specialty retail sporting goods store when she was just a teenager. It was a part-time job intended to provide her with a little spending money. But Caitlin turned out to be one of those amazing part-time people whom customers love and that provide real value for a store.

At first Caitlin was just excited to have a job. She was proud of the work she did and took care to learn all the product knowledge she could. Further, she dug in and learned about the store's customers—who they were and how they participated in their sport. Caitlin was also active in the sport and she thought it was great to have customers with shared interests. It was a real perk to be able to walk up to athletes and coaches at events and chat with them, and she even become friends with some.

In this age of online shopping, the specialty store is something that is becoming increasingly rare. This particular store was an independent retail location, serving a niche market. This type of store relies on repeat business and referrals. Therefore, having salespeople who develop a strong relationship with customers was key to the store's success. Caitlin was one of those people. Customers loved her and they trusted her knowledge and expertise. She knew her stuff and had an established customer base as well as a solid reputation that won her continuous referrals.

Caitlin had an extremely strong work ethic. Even if customer traffic was slow, she always found something to do. Her point of view was if customer traffic and sales were low, then there was no excuse for the store not to be in perfect shape. She spent her quiet time cleaning, stocking shelves, and rearranging inventory.

Caitlin frequently worked overtime to complete backlogs of work left by other employees. However, she infrequently billed for it. If she did bill for it, she would be met with annoyance from the owner. The owner seemed to expect multiple days' worth of work to get done, as well as high sales and customer service, in the space of one shift.

It was the norm for Caitlin to work alone in the store. There were times when the owner was also there, but mostly Caitlin was trusted to handle things herself. Being given a lot of autonomy was great, but it also meant there was no clear plan for how things should be done. Caitlin would spend hours doing tasks the owner had assigned, only to come in for her next shift and see all her hard work had been undone—often by the very person who had assigned the task. This left her feeling as if her work wasn't valued. Over time, Caitlin was frequently irked by how inconsiderate this felt, because she took so much pride in her work. It started to chafe on her that the owner expected her to do the work of three people, but she certainly wasn't getting paid that way. Caitlin did get some pay raises over time, but then she would learn new people just coming in were being paid the same, or even more, than she was.

After working for the store for several years, Caitlin finally decided it was time to leave. She had plans to travel overseas and used this as her reason to quit. Although that was why she left, the reason she didn't want to return to that job was because of the lack of respect and consideration the owner had shown her.

## So, what happened?

Caitlin's strong work ethic led her to sort of take on the role of manager. The store needed more hierarchy—it needed a manager, and the other staff and customers certainly viewed Caitlin as such.

There was no one specific event that led Caitlin to want to leave the store. Rather, there was a gradual decline in her job satisfaction over time. She began to feel that what she did no longer mattered to the owner. Good ideas she put forward were "stolen" by the owner, and Caitlin didn't get the credit she felt she deserved. She received no consideration for her creativity and care for the store's well-being. This prompted Caitlin to start hoarding her ideas and implementing them on her own, so people would know it was done by her.

With very little communication coming from the owner, things were often a surprise to Caitlin and the other staff. Caitlin was the only staff member who stayed long-term with the store. Others had come in, received no training, and were left to figure things out for themselves, eventually quitting out of frustration. Caitlin pitched in and tried to train. However, as she was often on shifts by herself, she didn't get much opportunity to teach others what she knew. As a result, things were often in a mess when Caitlin came in to work.

It was clear to Caitlin that expectations of her were very high, even unrealistic, and recognition and appreciation for this just wasn't there. There were so many times her work was ignored or re-done, and Caitlin has no desire to ever return to the store. She's not even sure she'd want to be a customer. At present, she avoids situations where she could possibly run into her old boss.

## What did she wish would have happened?

As an employee at the store for many years, Caitlin would have liked some acknowledgement and respect for her seniority. The other staff and customers all recognized Caitlin's contributions, but the store owner didn't seem to appreciate her. Caitlin considered it a slap in the face when the owner chose a new (part-time) employee as the "go-to person." Caitlin was hurt and confused. Perhaps if there had been an explanation of why Caitlin was given senior-employee responsibilities but treated as a junior, she would have understood. But the lack of communication and feedback left her in the dark as to why she was overlooked for promotion and recognition.

Some appreciation, consistency, and professionalism displayed by the owner would have gone a long way to making Caitlin feel proud of where she worked. She was very proud of the work she did and treated the store as if it was her own. However, Caitlin was often aware of the lack of stability and sense of what is important to the business that the owner displayed.

In short, what Caitlin really wanted was some consideration and recognition for her work and ideas, and to be treated as if she was a valued employee.

## What is a manager to do?

Managers should treat their employees as they would like to be treated.

It's often the case that part-time employees cause grief for their managers. In retail, especially, turnover is high and it's challenging to get great staff. According to LinkedIn, the retail sector had the second-highest rate of turnover in 2017.[1] Knowing this, it's all the more reason for Caitlin's manager to value her and try to retain her. Caitlin displayed knowledge, skill, care for the customers and the store, professionalism, and loyalty. It's understandable that she expected the same in return. Managers can learn from this. When they have a valuable employee, they should do what they can to keep them engaged and show them they are valued and respected. Frequent one on ones and consistent communication will help managers understand what makes the employee tick—what makes them want to come to work, do a great job, and pull in revenue as a result.

By knowing what drives an employee, a manager can tailor jobs to employee strengths. When people are given the opportunity to focus on jobs that leverage their strengths, they really blossom. They produce great work and are excited by what they do.

Managers who encourage collaboration amongst their staff will often be rewarded with some creative and inspiring ideas. When that happens, managers should acknowledge those ideas (publicly, if possible) and attribute them to the employee who generated them. Again, this falls into the area of consideration and respect. How would a manager feel if their ideas were claimed by others? That's how their employees would feel.

Create the kind of working environment where people feel valued and respected. Give your employees responsibility then recognize and pay them accordingly. Share what is important to the business and support them in their efforts to achieve their goals.

## Lessons learned

Working with a manager who fails to support employees will ultimately affect performance. Open communication and sharing ideas is a key to success.

- Managers should set up a system of communication for their staff. If they have people working different shifts, consider how best to keep them in the loop. Managers should demonstrate to them the importance they place on communication and encourage them to provide feedback.

- Managers should treat their employees as if they are valued. They should hold regular one on ones so as to learn more about them. In these sessions, relationships will be developed and valuable insight into how employees think and feel will be gained. This will help in support and encouragement moving forward.

- Managers should acknowledge accomplishments and success. People will do great work when they know they have a supportive and encouraging environment.

- Managers should recognize and attribute great work appropriately. They should connect employees' ideas to the success of the business and give them kudos for their contributions. This leads to employee engagement and feeling like part of a team.

- Managers should train their employees—both when they start and throughout their tenure with the business. When people feel underprepared or out of their element, they can be intimated and not want to be there. A good training program will help them be as prepared as possible to perform at peak levels for the company, and will encourage them to stay and grow in their roles.

- Managers should acknowledge what their employees have done well in their regular one on ones and point out how that is helping them grow and succeed. People are motivated by a sense of progression.

- Managers should be clear and concise in communication, especially when giving instructions for tasks to be carried out. If instructions are not clear, it's understandable that employees will put their own interpretation on things.

- Managers should be considerate of the contributions employees are making to the business. When employees are doing good work, managers shouldn't undo everything without providing a compelling reason.

# TOM

Tom was a corporate trainer, working under contract with a training vendor. He answered a job posting on Craigslist, and had a response within an hour from the company. Tom thought this was "pretty cool," and was impressed by how responsive the company was.

He was invited to come in for a week-long train-the-trainer session, during which he was trained in how the company liked their people to present themselves when working with customers. Although he wasn't paid to attend the training, Tom felt he got value out of it. After all, he was receiving a certificate program free of charge! The training was delivered by one of the people working with the company, and included a component during which the participants were required to conduct a presentation. Halfway though Tom's presentation, the owner of the company walked in. Tom had never met her before, but right away it was clear who was the centre of attention in the room. Tom continued his presentation under the scrutiny of this new arrival, and then was critiqued by her once he was done. It was a positive experience, and Tom felt he was positioned well to learn some very valuable things from someone with such energy.

Tom worked as a contractor, getting paid an hourly rate for the time he spent on company business. He was brought in as a trainer/facilitator but quickly moved up to course development. It was an exciting time, as he was learning a lot from the company owner, who worked closely with him. Eventually he was moved into a project manager role, and that is where Tom finally started to feel a little overwhelmed. He did not have any project management experience, and asked for training to help him out with this. As the owner of the company was a certified project manager, he felt she would have much knowledge to share with him.

The project management training never manifested, and Tom was left to figure it out for himself. About this same time, Tom's paycheck bounced. He was issued a new check immediately, and Tom thought no more of it … until the pattern repeated itself. It was clear the company was having money concerns, so it wasn't a surprise when Tom was asked to take a pay cut. He agreed and stayed on. After all, he needed the job and was learning a lot. It seemed worth it to take the risk.

After a short while, the office was moved to a location that was quite a bit farther away for Tom. He now had a much longer commute. However, there were a lot of big plans for the business, and some new people had started, so things seemed to be on an upswing. The new office was very nice, and there were some decorative touches which were professional and would no doubt be impressive to potential clients.

Tom was asked to move to a different pay structure, and he was paid by project when certain milestones were completed. Tom wasn't very pleased about this new structure, but went along with it anyway. He felt he had little choice, and the company owed him thousands of dollars at that point.

Tom was faced with supporting other staff members who were also disappointed with how things were going. In spite of Tom's personal situation, he was there to provide support and guidance for others, and even encouraged them to stick with the company. His own situation was shaky, but he was still a cheerleader for the company and felt there was potential. Yes, cheques were bouncing, but he believed the owner when she told him she would make things up to him later, when the company was in better financial shape.

One weekend, Tom and his wife were out on a day trip. The phone rang, and Tom was called into the office because he had supposedly missed some deliverables. This didn't make sense to Tom. He had spoken to the client recently, and all was on track. His boss seemed furious and would not believe that Tom had successfully completed the job the client wanted. She insisted he cut his day trip short and go into the office to fix things. The next business day, Tom spoke with the client, who was unaware there was any problem. According to him, all was fine.

It was becoming abundantly clear this was not a good place for Tom to be. His boss would say nice things to Tom, but then would belittle him at the same time. She would talk over him and never really listen to Tom's side of things. At times she would sing his praises, and at other times she would publicly berate him. Tom felt like he was in over his head, and needed clarification—which never came. His boss was more concerned with how things looked than with substance, and the staff felt like she failed as a boss. People were quitting at a rapid pace, which meant Tom had even more work on his plate.

There was a lack of consistency and communication. Tom's boss would make unrealistic promises to clients, which would leave Tom scrambling to keep up. There was a great deal of stress, and not even the promise of a reliable paycheck to make up for it. In spite of the fact that Tom was owed thousands of dollars, he decided to cut his losses and quit after not quite two years of being with the company.

## So, what happened?

Tom decided he was through with putting himself out there for a company that was not delivering on its promises. It was clear he couldn't trust them to deliver on their promises to him as an employee, and he worried they treated customers the same way. From Tom's point of view, it wasn't just the company's reputation at stake, but his as well.

Money was important to Tom; he needed the job. But it was more than that which caused him to quit. Tom felt the company was morally responsible to come through for its employees and customers. Tom couldn't trust them any longer. If they couldn't keep their word about paychecks, why should he trust them about his money or anything else?

Certainly, Tom learned a lot while working for the company. He worked hard and made progress, having achieved a couple of promotions during his tenure. Although this forward momentum was exciting, Tom didn't have the support and training he needed to succeed in the job. The result was he often felt in over his head.

As a trainer, Tom's boss was very good—one of the best he'd ever seen. However, as a boss she left a lot to be desired. At times she would sing the praises of her employees, and at other times she would say terrible things. She was unpredictable, and Tom never knew what to expect when he went in to work or answered her calls.

## What did he wish would have happened?

It might seem obvious that Tom would have liked to be paid for the work he did—regularly and consistently. But, believe it or not, that is not why he quit.

Near the end of his time with the company, the owner called Tom and tore a strip off of him. She claimed he didn't deliver as expected. It was insulting, because in Tom's mind, she was the one who didn't deliver. Tom would really have appreciated clear and consistent directions. He had requested help to expand his knowledge of project management (something his boss was in an ideal situation to provide), and really wished that had transpired.

Tom also wanted his boss to trust that he was doing good work. It is often said that trust is something you earn. Tom honestly felt the work he delivered was good, and since he had earned the trust of the clients, why did the owner not believe in him? To make things worse, the reason was never communicated to him.

Clear communication would have answered Tom's questions about what success looked like and how it was best delivered. Had his boss explained clearly what her expectations were, Tom would have been able to achieve them. However, he always felt as if success was a moving target, and he never felt confident he would reach that target.

## What is a manager to do?

What are the takeaways from this story? Certainly, communication is a large part of it—managers must communicate regularly with their people.

Most employees are not mind-readers. Many are not even slightly intuitive. If managers would like their people to do something, they should clearly and concisely define and communicate what is to be done. Further, managers must be consistent in their approach to employees. By being mercurial and changing direction seemingly on a whim, managers leave their employees unsure of what will happen next, and afraid of the consequences. This behaviour is extremely difficult for employees to take day in and day out, and as a result, they will look for a more stable work situation, with a more stable and consistent person to report to.

In Simone's story, we saw a clear example of workplace bullying. Tom's story is also one of being bullied, but it's not as obvious. Because Tom's boss would sometimes build him up, he would feel cared for and appreciated. However, each time the nasty side would rear up, Tom would feel uncared for, confused, belittled, attacked, and very stressed out as a result. When employees are watching their backs and preparing for the next blow, how can they put their best foot forward or trust their manager?

When managers don't trust their employees, there is an effect on the results achieved. When trust is high, people tend to rise to the occasion, being more productive, communicating better, collaborating more effectively, and being all-around more engaged in their work. They are willing to take risks and are, as a result, more creative. This can lead to extraordinary insights, collaboration, and innovation.

When trust is low, the opposite occurs. Employees play it safe, because they are afraid of failing and incurring the wrath of their bosses. Productivity is reduced and time to task completion is increased, because employees are constantly checking and double-checking everything before presenting a finished product. When trust is low, creativity is decreased. Who wants to try to innovate in a risky environment? It's much better to take the safest route.

Employees are looking for someone to lead them and show them how things are best done. They need someone to provide direction and help them to understand the "why" around what they're doing. When managers are nice and supportive one minute and angry and blaming the next, it's difficult for their people to trust them. Constantly changing direction for no clear reason leaves employees unsure of how to proceed. If they can clearly understand why the change is occurring and put their faith in their manager to lead them in the new direction, employees will go along for the ride. If not, they're going to look for someone else to ride along with.

It should be obvious that employees need to trust they will be fairly compensated for the services they provide the company. This includes being able to trust that they *will* be paid. Bouncing paychecks is a sure way to lose employees. They will eventually be forced to find a company that will pay them. After all, they have bills too. In tough times, businesses often face difficulties making payroll. If you can't do it, then tell your people ahead of time so that they can make appropriate arrangements. They'll likely leave you, but telling them is the right thing to do. Laying off staff for this reason is something that happens in the business world. When it happens, employees are sad (sometimes devastated), but they do understand. It's a much better approach than making empty promises and owing them thousands of dollars that will never get paid. I'm no lawyer, but I believe that's also illegal.

## Lessons learned

Establishing, growing, extending, and restoring trust is a key leadership competency.[1]

- Managers should clearly and concisely communicate what the direction of the company is. From there, they should communicate the vision for the department, team, and project. If employees understand the "why" and the "how" of what they're working on and for, they can better produce what is needed.

- Managers should explain the "how." Employees are far more engaged when they understand what they are working on. Clarity of instruction, of how to execute, and of why this needs to be done will contribute greatly to engagement.

- Managers should trust their team members. Trust is one of the most powerful forms of motivation.[2] People want to be trusted—they thrive on trust. If managers want their reports to give their best, they should trust they'll do their best to deliver.

- Managers should be trustworthy. Their people rely on them to lead, and managers have to deliver the goods. If they can't trust their manager, employees will leave.

- Managers should be truthful. Lying or hiding the truth can damage relationships greatly. When people lie, they destroy trust. If there is a lack of trust, employees won't band together with the company during tough times to work it through. Rather, they'll abandon ship and look for something else they hope will be better.

- Managers should pay people fairly for the work they do. If they can't pay them, then perhaps they shouldn't have employees. Managers might have to take on the load themselves and let their employees go on to other opportunities.

# Part 2:
# The Overarching Theme

## THE OVERARCHING THEME

In listening and in writing down what these seven people told me, I was struck by a theme that ran throughout all their situations. In every one of these stories, there was a decided lack of **respect** shown to the employees.

When I was writing the content for this book, a particular song kept running through my mind. I bet you can even guess what it was—"Respect," written by Otis Redding and the signature song for the late, great Aretha Franklin.

*All I'm askin' for is a little respect*

I'll admit, I was a little surprised at what people wished would have happened in each of their experiences. I expected at least a few of them to say they wanted more money. After all, most of us would really love to make more money, and a great many of us feel we're underpaid. However, study after study shows that money isn't a key driver of engagement.

According to Gallup's study on Employee Engagement, people don't leave their jobs—they leave their managers. Research shows that 50% of Americans have left a job to *"get away from their manager at some point in their career."*[1] This is a shockingly large number, yet the stories I presented back it up. The people who told their stories all left their jobs because of managers who didn't engage them or engage *with* them. It's likely that the managers themselves weren't engaged. Here are statistics for engagement amongst the workforce:

- Gallup's study found that only 30% of the workforce is engaged in North America. Globally that number stands at about 15%.

- Gallup also found that only 35% of managers are engaged.

So maybe it's a chicken and egg thing … employees are not engaged because their managers are not making work interesting and engaging; and managers don't make efforts to make the workplace interesting and engaging because they don't really want to be there, either.

Perhaps if managers could make their teams happier, the workplace would be more engaging, and as a result, the type of place they'd all like to be.

Here is what RESPECT means to me:

# IT'S NOT THEM, IT'S YOU

**R — RELATIONSHIP**
Take time to develop relationships with your team members. Learn what makes them tick—what are they passionate about? What motivates them? Great managers build relationships that create trust, open dialogue and full transparency.

**E — EMPATHY**
By emphasizing a culture of empathy and caring, organizations can expect better results in terms of employee satisfaction and reduced costs from absenteeism, burnout, or turnover.

**S — SUPPORT**
Create a supportive environment. If you want your people to be creative and bring forth ideas, then you must have a safe space for them to do so. If you punish or taunt them when they fail, they will, understandably, be reluctant to take any future risks.

**P — PROMOTION**
Opportunities for advancement is in the top 3 motivators for employees. So are better compensation and benefits. Understand your employees' career goals, and act as an advocate for them within the company.

**E — EMPOWERMENT**
Trust employees to do their best work, make good decisions, and choose what will work. It may not be exactly what you would do, but it can still work. Empowering employees to do good work their way will lead to them feeling strong, capable, and engaged.

**C — CONSIDERATION**
Be considerate of the contributions your employees are giving to the business. In your regular one-on-ones, acknowledge what they have done well, and point out how that is helping them to grow and succeed.

**T — TRUST**
Lying or hiding the truth can damage relationships greatly.
As managers, we have to be trustworthy. Our people rely on us to lead them, and we have to deliver the goods. If they can't trust us, they'll leave.

# Part 3: What To Do

## WHAT YOU CAN DO ABOUT IT

*R-E-S-P-E-C-T,
find out what it means to me...
- Otis Redding*

In this section, we'll dig deeper into the concepts presented above. Each of the seven concepts—Relationship, Empathy, Support, Promotion, Empowerment, Consideration, and Trust—relate to what keeps employees engaged in their work. The lack of these things, as we've seen, has them heading for the door.

The good news for managers behaving badly is that things can be turned around.

# RELATIONSHIPS

Every company wants to be successful. Guess what—the people who work in those companies want to be successful, too. Both company leaders, and the people who report to them, want to feel they are working toward a common goal. But how do employees know what the goal is, if their manager is not communicating with them?

The world's best companies truly excel in the products and technology that make them successful. But underpinning all of that is the people who are doing the work. These same best companies go beyond the technology and put focus on human interactions. They may use vehicles such as job exchanges, mentoring, social networks, and other programs, but the common thread is the conversations they're having about the growth and development of the employees.

In *Why Should Anyone Be Led by You?*[1] we learn that leadership must be viewed as a relationship between leaders and those who follow them. Leaders must inspire their people with a sense of purpose or belonging. To do that, they need to develop relationships. In order to develop these relationships, managers must communicate thoughtfully and consistently.

Communicating thoughtfully doesn't mean walking on eggshells. Rather, it means understanding the team members—what drives them, how best to reach them, and the message itself. Additionally, the manager needs to understand their own personal strengths and weaknesses, for example, how do they communicate (or not)? We live in a time where there are so many communication options immediately available (face-to-face, video chat, phone, social media, email, etc.), it's easy for a manager to think they've gotten across whatever messages they need to get out there. They can send an email, or have a flash meeting, and that should take care of communication, right? That may very well take care of things in the short term. However, employees need more. They need the kind of communication that tells them *why* they should do what they're being asked to do. What's in it for the company, the department, the team ... and them. That kind of communication demands something more in-depth than an email.

People are drawn to leaders who are good at communicating what they believe, and who make their employees feel special, safe, and part of something bigger. They feel a bond with the manager and with the organization.[2] Once employees feel this way, they are much more likely to be engaged with the company and the work they do.

Managers have a huge impact on employee engagement. According to Gallup's State of the American Manager report, a mere 30% of American workers are engaged. Most of that shocking statistic is due to a lack of relationship with the employees' managers. One in two employees has left a job just to get away from a bad manager. That was certainly the case in the stories presented earlier. In each and every case, the employees left the organization because of their managers. Each of those people began their role as excited, driven workers who brought much to their organizations. They were productive and talented—the kinds of people companies want to attract, not lose.

Why should we worry about engaging employees? Gallup has found that when a company raises its employee engagement levels, everything gets better: productivity, quality, lower turnover, less absenteeism, and fewer safety incidents. In addition, companies with highly engaged employees report having higher revenue and customer satisfaction.

However, most managers aren't creating the type of environment in which employees feel comfortable, never mind motivated or engaged. As we learned from Rosalie, Percy, and all the others, having a bad manager can make people feel miserable at work, and that feeling often follows them home, affecting their personal lives and overall stress levels.

There are real costs tied to disengagement. Gallup tells us that an actively disengaged employee (one who is "unhappy and unproductive at work and liable to spread negativity to coworkers") can cost their organization $3,400 for every $10,000 of salary (34%). This means if you have an actively disengaged employee making $60,000 a year, your company will incur associated costs of $20,400 per year.[4] I'm sure most managers would be reluctant to let something slide that loses them tens of thousands of dollars per year, so this statistic should be making them think about engagement.

Employee behaviour has an impact on company performance, since many employees have at least some control over how hard they work. The extent to which employees trust they will be treated fairly and honestly by their managers may influence how much effort they put into their work. As a result, the degree of trust employees feel toward their managers will impact company performance.[5] Studies have found there is a positive relationship between workplace performance (financial, productivity, product, or service quality) and trust. In other words, if employees trust their managers, they will work harder and be more productive. If they don't trust their managers, they will do poorer quality work and will eventually leave the company.

### So, how can managers turn that around?

Success in business begins with success in employee/manager relationships, which begins with communication. Communication is the root of trust. Trust affects the quality of relationships, communication, individual effort, and work quality. It's highly important that we take the time to develop relationships with our team members, and the best way to do this is in regular and frequent one on ones.

Gallup finds that great managers build the type of relationships that create trust, open dialogue, and full transparency. Consistent communication, regardless of how it happens, is tied to higher engagement. Those employees who meet regularly with their managers are almost three times more likely to be engaged than employees who do not.

# IT'S NOT THEM, IT'S YOU

This is a sobering thought, because if engagement is only at 30%, that means there are a lot of employees out there who don't have regular meetings with their bosses. Engagement is highest among those employees who have daily interaction with their managers (face-to-face, phone, email). Those managers who meet face-to-face with their people regularly are generally the most successful at engaging employees.

It's pretty clear that managers need to make time in their schedules for regular, frequent, and consistent communication with their team members.

## One on ones

One on ones are the best way for managers to discuss issues, develop relationships, and connect with their employees. They are the best way to ensure company and employee goals are being met. One on ones also afford the manager an opportunity to provide feedback and coaching, and to share knowledge about what's coming down the pike for the department and the organization. Perhaps most importantly, one on ones give the manager the opportunity to do a pulse check on the employee's morale and stress level. Are they happy and productive? Or are they a flight risk?

One on ones should be held, at minimum, once per month. Ideally, they'll be held more frequently than that, like once per week. Managers often cite lack of time as the reason they don't engage in frequent one on ones, but as we've seen throughout the course of this book, it's so important to give your employees time with you. Ultimately, the time invested pays off decidedly, with greater transparency, awareness of project status, closer bonds with team members, and understanding what drives them. As we learned, it also pays off financially. Engaged employees are more productive, and cost the company less than disengaged employees.

Most one on one meetings should last about thirty minutes. That amount of time allows for a little personal connecting, some time for your messages, and some time for reviewing employee development goals. The first few meetings might take longer than thirty minutes, because there is a lot of ground to cover to bring you both up-to-date. But it doesn't take long to fall into a half-hour cadence. Be sure to allow a little cushion in your schedule in case things run overtime. You don't want to jeopardize a good discussion because you have something else you have to tend to.

In that thirty minutes, allow approximately ten minutes to talk about the employee's needs, ten minutes to talk about the manager's concerns, and ten minutes to talk about employee development.

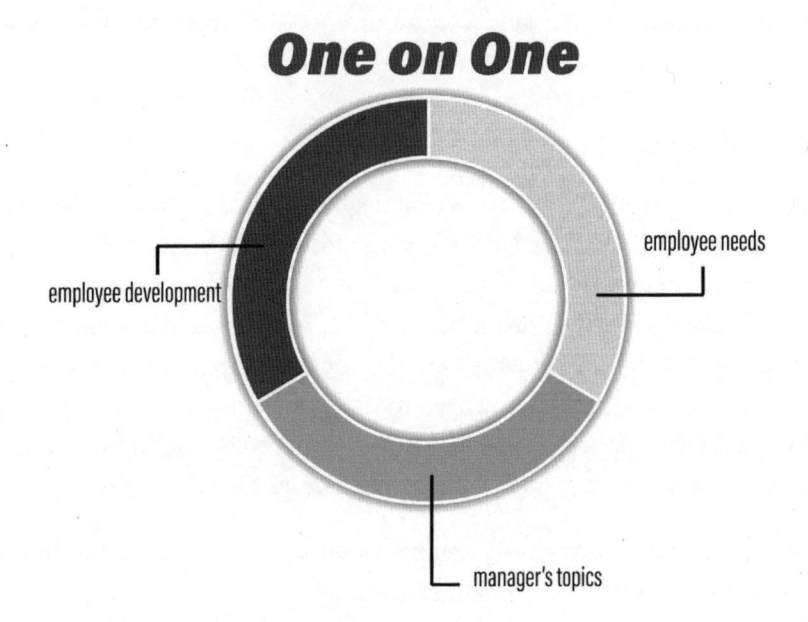

**One on One**

- employee development
- employee needs
- manager's topics

Set up a recurring schedule and commit to it. As we read in Rosalie's story, the manager would often skip out on weekly one on ones without communicating anything. This left Rosalie feeling forgotten and ignored. She also felt that any relationship with her manager was tenuous, at best. Trust was pretty much non-existent.

If you and your team are committed to regular meetings, it'll be harder to procrastinate. In time, you will all come to rely on one on ones and the information that is shared in those meetings. There are times when you may have to cancel. That's okay—stuff happens. Honour the commitment and reschedule the one on one. That is a strong indicator of how important the meeting, and by extension, the employee is to you.

It's crucial to put the meetings into your calendar, so they don't accidentally get forgotten or scheduled over. Make the appointments recurring and invite the employee.

The sessions should be somewhat informal. After all, it's a check-in, not a performance appraisal. Managers don't need to have a fixed agenda, but they should have some talking points prepared. Put yourself in the mindset that this will be casual and relaxed. Encourage your people to prepare ahead of time as well, and to bring forward any specific ideas and issues they'd like to discuss. You might even want to reach out ahead of time to see if there are any specific topics you can prepare for. Most of all, remember this meeting is for the employee (mostly), so put the focus on what they want to discuss.

Meetings don't have to be held in an office. Why not go for a coffee, or have a walking meeting? The change of pace will set a nice tone for the conversation.

## Prepping for the one on one

As mentioned above, this is a casual meeting, so you don't need a firm plan going in. It is helpful, however, to plan a few things to talk about, especially if it's important you communicate those items to your team member.

Be personal—your people want to know something about you, and likewise, you about them. That way it feels more as if they are working *with* you, not *for* you. This doesn't mean you have to be their best friend. It does mean you should consider they are people, not just workers. Know a little bit about them and allow them to learn a little about you. Here are some easy ways you can accomplish that:

- Ask them what their plans are for the weekend.
- Ask them how their weekend was.
- Eat lunch with them.
- Share something about yourself.

Sometimes you'll have team members who don't choose to share anything personal about themselves. That's okay. Allow them to dictate the course of the conversation. If they only want to talk about work, then talk about work. Remember, they need to trust you if they're going to disclose personal things about themselves. You may not yet have earned their trust. As you develop your relationship with them, they might open up a little. When they do, be ready to share a little of yourself, too.

To build loyalty and create the right opportunities for employees, managers need to:

- Help develop them by supporting training they request.
- Give them interesting work that clearly aligns with the company goals.
- Communicate with them consistently.
- Listen to them.
- Show respect.
- Build trust and openness.

With this in mind, plan a couple of topics for discussion that will lead them into one of the areas listed above. Here are some questions you can consider opening with:

*What's happening in your world?*

*It's a really busy time right now; what kinds of things are occupying your thoughts?*

*How is life treating you lately?*

These open-ended questions could take the conversation in many directions, so be prepared to have a deeper conversation.

## Some topics for a one on one

Even though one on ones can be about nearly anything, it's smart to have a few topics for discussion prepared.

1.  **How Do They Work?**

    In order to better support your team members in their efforts, it's smart to know how they work. Try asking questions like this:

    - When are you most productive during your day?
    - Where do you prefer to work?
    - How do you prefer to work?
    - What do you do when you get stuck on something?
    - How can I help?

2.  **Making a Connection**

    If you hope to have effective one on one conversations, you will need to connect with your team member. The best way to accomplish this is to listen—really listen—to what they're saying. As they open up to you, demonstrate that you care about them and what they're saying. This goes a long way toward establishing trust.

    Start the meeting by giving your team member a chance to share what's on their mind. Listen more than you speak during this time. Most people like to talk about themselves, so give them a chance to do so. By showing genuine interest, you'll encourage them to open up to you. Ask some questions about what they like to do, and look for common ground. When you find something you both share, you can use that as a springboard to develop a rapport. Even if it's just that you both wish the weather was nicer can help to start a conversation.

    Here are some questions you can try to start making a connection:

    - What can I do to help you?
    - How do you think we could work better together?

- Whose opinions do you respect? What have they done to make you feel this way?
- What's the most exciting thing you're working on? Why?
- What are you passionate about?

3. **Happiness**

   Some managers may find this hard to believe, but personal happiness has a big impact on productivity and engagement. There are managers among us who think it should be enough for employees to collect a paycheck and that alone should make them want to come to work and do a good job. But that industrial-revolution way of thinking really doesn't apply anymore.

   Employees go through the recruitment and hiring process with the promise of all the good things that await them when they go to work for a company. They're wooed by the ideas of a paycheck, recognition, promotions, fun coworkers, and all those extra perks companies pile on to attract talent (pizza lunches, free beer, Ping-Pong tables, etc.). But mostly what they're looking for is to be successful. If they can be a success, then surely they'll be happy, right? The trouble is, bad managers can get in the way of the employee's success, and as a result, happiness. Once this happens, they stop pouring their energy into their work, and spend their days doing only what they have to do to get the job done. For some managers this may be enough. But most managers would really love for their people to do their best work, culminating in increased productivity, customer satisfaction, and profits. Bad managers can make employees lose all passion for the job, and eventually look for the next promising opportunity.

---

*I've learned that making a "living" is not the same thing as making a "life".* —Maya Angelou

---

How much does happiness affect productivity? Studies show that productivity increases by an average of 12%, and as much as 20%, when workers are happy. Conversely, real-world problems, such as grief and family matters, have an adverse effect on workers. Unhappiness and decreased productivity are found to have a causal link.[6]

Happiness is something we all want, and since we spend such a large part of our lives at work, it makes sense we'd like to be happy at work. Take the opportunity provided in the one on one to see how happy your team members are, and learn how they could be happier at work.

- Are you happy working here?
- Is there anyone on the team who you find difficult to work with? Why is that?
- What kind of projects do you like to work on?
- Do you feel valued at work? Why or why not?

4. **Significant Projects and Action Items**

Your people will want to update you on their progress with their projects, and you'll want to know that as well. So, ask them what they're doing and what you need to know. Include any issues and challenges they may be facing. Review tasks and milestones and check how on-track they are with project deliverables. Take this opportunity to offer help, support, and resources if needed.

- Tell me about the projects you're working on.
- Are we on track?
- What roadblocks are you dealing with?
- Do you have everything you need to complete the tasks?

5. **Goals–Short- and Long-term**

People like to work toward and achieve goals. So, work with your team members on setting reasonable goals, and support them in their progress. By speaking to them about how they are doing with their goals, you will keep on top of their progress as well. After all, it's important to your department, and to the organization on the whole, that progress toward targets is being made.

Short-term goals are those that can be completed within a shorter time frame, e.g., one year. These goals are important to keeping projects on task. Long-term goals are those carried out over longer time frames. They are important to the company, but they are also very important to the employee's sense of fulfillment on the job. Learn what your employees' goals are. Help them with setting goals, and with breaking down large, long-term goals into smaller, shorter-term goals that are easier to manage.

- What are your goals for the week/month?
- How do they tie into the larger, departmental goals?
- Where are the bottlenecks? How can I help you to deal with them?
- What do you want to achieve?
- How is the work you're doing contributing to the goals?

6. **Coaching and Support**

The one on one is a perfect time to help employees understand what they're good at and how their strengths contribute to team success. Coach your people to help develop skills that would contribute to their success and/or job satisfaction. Reinforce that you're there to help them.

- How can I help you?
- What is frustrating you right now?
- Would you like coaching? With what?
- What would you like to learn about?

Thoughtful questions are powerful tools. Imagine what you can learn when you ask them, especially since many people are hesitant to share much about themselves until they're asked.

---

*59% of millennial employees who strongly agree that they can talk with their managers about "non-work-related issues" are engaged at work. —Gallup*

---

## During the one on one

Make the tone of one on ones informal and relaxed. This might be tough at times. It takes a long time for employees to relax into meetings with their boss if they've had a career's worth of appraisals and reviews.

Go into it with the right mindset. Look at it this way—how do you feel when you're summoned into your boss's office? You could be excused if you would feel a bit anxious or worried about what you did wrong. Your team members may be feeling the same anxiety, until you assure them through your behaviour in the one on one that this is meant to be a check-in, and is about them. At the first meeting especially, your employee will be wondering what's about to happen. To set them at ease, ask a few questions and listen carefully to the responses. Hold a conversation, not an inquisition. When you listen to the responses, you'll learn more about what makes your employee tick. Make a decision to use this time to learn about your employees, what challenges they face, and what you can do to support them.

Make sure you are holding the conversation in a private place, where coworkers can't easily hear what's being said. Consider going to a coffee shop nearby, go for lunch, or even take a walk and talk at the same time. The change in environment will make this meeting seem less like a review and more conversational.

Be sure to make a point of sharing "good news" stories and celebrating accomplishments. It's always nice to recognize what's going well, and the positive energy will set a nice tone for the meeting. Resist the urge to make the discussion about project and task updates. Sure, those things will come up, but the real purpose of the meeting is to find out what is going on with the employee and develop a relationship with them. So, ask questions, listen to responses, and learn about your employee.

From time to time, your employee might have challenges that might hold them back or derail a project. Resist the urge to jump in with a solution. After all, these meetings are about *developing* your employees as well. You can ask leading questions and guide them to solutions. They will be much more likely to be engaged in the process, because they feel they're in charge and are contributing value. You should also offer coaching and support to assist them in overcoming hurdles.

One on ones also provide a great opportunity for managers to get feedback about what employees do and how they are doing it. Why not ask what you can do to help them be more productive? No doubt there are things you can learn about managing them, and the relaxed environment of a well-run one on one will help them to open up.

Be sure to take notes during the discussion. Doing so demonstrates you care about what they have to say. It also helps you to create an action item list, which will be a good jumping off point for your next one on one. At least for the first meeting, ask permission to take notes and explain why you're doing so. That should allay any concerns your team member may have.

What if you cover everything you both wanted to talk about and there's still time left according to the schedule? There's nothing saying you have to end early. Use the remaining time to chat. Get to know one another better, talk about fun things, and dream up ideas for future projects (or future staff events). You've reserved the time for the employee, and nothing will say more about how valuable they are than if you spend quality time genuinely getting to know them rather than rushing to get back to other tasks. Conversely, it's okay to end the meeting early and allow everyone to get back to jobs that await if there's nothing left to be said. Drawing out the meeting with nothing much to say can be awkward and pretty darned uncomfortable.

If you do this well, your employees will leave the one on one feeling heard and understood—a great feeling for anyone to experience. If employees feel their manager—and by extension, their company—cares, they will feel supported and inclined to do great work.

## After the one on one

There's a reason that managers should take notes during one on ones.

If the conversation flows, no doubt there will be some great ideas that come out of the one on one. If you've been making notes all along, it'll be easy for you to refer back to them and summarize what you've discussed and agreed to. Make plans about who is doing what, and by when. Let your team member know you'll be following up on what was discussed, and commit to doing so within a certain time frame.

It's important for managers to be organized after the one on one. Send a recap of the meeting. Point out the main things that were discussed, key takeaways, and next steps. This way you're both accountable for outcomes, and the employees will know you've taken the whole thing seriously.

Ask the employee whether your recap is in line with what they took from the discussion. Make sure they're comfortable with the next steps outlined.

What is the employee accountable for?

What is the manager accountable for?

Most importantly, take action on what was discussed. Nothing you talk about in the one on one means anything if you don't take action. For example, if you promised to send links to websites or provide information, be sure to do so. If you offered to coach them once per week, start setting the meetings.

Remember that one on one meetings are about developing relationships with your team members. You don't want to have the type of relationship where they feel they can't trust you, or that you are disinterested in what they are doing. Any promises made during the one on one must be acted upon in order for the manager to remain credible and trustworthy.[7]

## Still not convinced a one on one is worth your time?

Need some more convincing that frequent and regular one on ones are a good idea? Here are some final reasons to incorporate them into what you do:[8]

- You can choose not to have one on ones and continue communicating via email. However, this leads to a full inbox, and a lot of important details might be skipped. In the end, this inefficient method of communication can cost managers much more time than a recurring thirty-minute face-to-face meeting.

- Your team members will still need to talk to you, so they'll hang around outside your office door or flag you down as you walk by their desks. At the very least, you'll be distracted and not fully ready to absorb what they're telling you. Even worse, you're very likely to forget whatever it is they told you on the fly. This communication method isn't productive for anyone.

- Not having one on one discussions could mean the employee moves ahead on projects without adequate information and guidance. The end result could be a big mess that has to be cleaned up later.

- But what is worst is that without conducting one on one meetings, you've lost the opportunity to develop a positive relationship with your people. What you've done is sent the message that they're not really a priority. Needless to say, that leads to lower engagement, morale, and productivity … and makes employees more likely to leave.

## IT'S NOT THEM, IT'S YOU

On the next page is a template for the one on one conversation. It includes timing suggestions, sample questions you might like to use, and space for notes.

You can download a copy of this template from my company website at www.cchangelearning.com/resources.

# LAURA SUKOROKOFF

# One on One Conversations

Use this template as a framework for your weekly One on One conversations. Take notes in the space below, and refer back to your notes in future meetings.

### 10 MINUTES FOR THE EMPLOYEE
Discuss whatever the employee wants to discuss. This is an opportunity to learn about them and what they feel is most important.

### 10 MINUTES FOR THE MANAGER
Discuss projects in progress and what is upcoming. This is a good time to bring up any concerns and discuss tasks, etc. that need attention.

### 10 MINUTES FOR PROFESSIONAL DEVELOPMENT
Discuss where the employee would like to develop their knowledge, skills and abilities. Also discuss career plans (short and long term), and what is needed to get them there.

### SAMPLE QUESTIONS

- HOW'S YOUR DAY GOING?
- WHAT ARE YOUR PLANS FOR THE WEEKEND?
- WHAT'S NEW IN YOUR WORLD?
- IT'S A REALLY BUSY TIME RIGHT NOW. WHAT'S OCCUPYING YOUR THOUGHTS?

- WHAT ARE YOU WORKING ON NOW?
- HOW IS THAT GOING?
- WHERE CAN I HELP YOU?
- WHO DO YOU NEED TO WORK WITH ON THIS?

- WHAT DO YOU DO WHEN YOU GET STUCK ON SOMETHING?
- HOW CAN I SUPPORT YOU?
- WHERE DO YOU SEE YOURSELF IN A FEW YEARS?
- HOW CAN I HELP YOU GET THERE?
- WHAT KIND OF PROFESSIONAL DEVELOPMENT OPPORTUNITIES INTEREST YOU?

### notes

# EMPATHY

Most companies don't care. There, I've said it. Companies may think they care, and they may promote in advertising that they care, but their actions belie their words. Well, maybe I should adjust that statement a bit. Companies care a great deal about: profit, doing well for the shareholders, growth, and revenue. The people working in their companies and generating that revenue, on the other hand, tend to get left out of the caring equation.

Let me give you an example of this—I once heard a CEO speaking to the head of HR at an up-and-coming firm. The CEO was speaking about why they had complimentary coffee, tea, and snacks for the employees. It wasn't just that they were being nice and providing a perk. The real reason was so employees wouldn't lose productivity and waste time by going out for coffee or taking breaks. If snacks are provided, the employees can load up and head back to their desks, barely interrupting their workflow.

If the people running the companies and making the policies have this kind of attitude, it's small wonder their managers espouse that point of view. After all, they have to keep an eye on the things the company holds dear—profit, shareholder value, revenue, growth, etc.—and make sure their employees adhere to the policies.

I realize I sound like a cynic, but you don't have to go far to find evidence of this, just read company reviews on Glassdoor. You'll see there are a great many reviews posted where people talk about how the company and its leadership has let them down. If a company truly had a caring culture, there wouldn't be so many disengaged employees who are looking for new opportunities. There also wouldn't be so many managers behaving badly. After all, as Donald Trump famously says, "It's not personal, it's business."

I, for one, think work is very personal. The average person will spend about ninety thousand hours working in their lifetime—even more for some people. That's a huge number! Approximately one-third of our day is spent at work, and for most people that is the largest block of time they have to spend with other people. It makes sense that employees will look at the workplace as somewhere to make connections and develop relationships. Because we spend so much time with our coworkers, it's also someplace where we expect people will make an effort to understand us and sympathize with what we're going through.

Unfortunately, however, that is often not the case. At work we are expected to suck it up and deal. You may have heard the common statement, "It is what it is," meaning you just have to accept things the way they are; there is no perceived way to address the issue and there is no use in complaining. There are things to be done on behalf of the company, and they take priority. This kind of attitude creeps into the workplace and becomes the cultural norm.

Let me share a story with you. I once worked for a company that delivered training programs for a large, global sporting event. Upon starting with the company, the team was told there was going to be a lot of work to do, and everyone needed to care for themselves so they didn't fall sick. It was cold and flu season, and we were encouraged to stay home should we catch a bug. Sure enough, I fell ill with a terrible flu. I was very sick, and had to call in to beg out of the presentation I was scheduled to deliver that evening. I could barely get out of bed. How was I supposed to speak in front of two hundred people? Fortunately for me, I had colleagues who were well-versed in the material and I had faith they could cover for me. After all, I was supposed to stay home and not make everyone else sick, right? A little later during that day, I received a heads-up email from a colleague, advising me that our manager was furious and that she told my coworkers that I was faking illness because I was too nervous about the presentation. They, of course, assured her that was not the case, but the manager continued to rant about my not showing up. It was apparent to all that, although the corporate policy was for sick employees to stay home, the culture in that department and the attitude displayed by that manager was you were supposed to show up anyway. I dragged myself in the next day and carried on with working, in spite of being so ill that it took months for me to get through it. The message to all of us was very clear—the manager didn't care about us personally and was only concerned about getting the most from us, even if it negatively impacted our health.

This same message was displayed by the company Emily worked for. In her story, she reported to a manager who didn't seem to appreciate, at all, the pain she was experiencing as a result of her injuries. The company culture was to suck it up and deal. Because Emily didn't display any obvious symptoms, the assumption was the injury wasn't serious. When it became apparent it really was more severe than originally thought, and her work was impacted, the company and her team turned against Emily. It's often the thinking in companies that if people take time off to heal, they are lazy or untrustworthy. In the words of an English friend of mine, they are "skiving off" (avoiding going to work when they know they should).

Of course, there are people who take advantage of companies in this way. However, most people would prefer to be productive and useful, doing good work and being proud of their contributions. Why then do managers distrust their employees so? Have a few bad apples spoiled the whole bunch?

Most companies have personal or sick days available to their employees. According to the US Bureau of Labor Statistics, all full-time private sector employees have an average of eight days of paid sick leave available to them after one year of service. If you've been with the company for less than a year, you may be out of luck and any time off will be unpaid. In Canada, the decision to offer paid sick leave is left to the discretion of the company. In my experience, five paid sick days per year is a norm. However, almost 40% of private-sector employees in Canada have no paid sick leave—at all.[1] The end result of that is people continue to work through illness. They can't afford to take unpaid leave, so they power through, doing poor-quality work and affecting (and perhaps infecting) those they work with.

Being able to work from home is a big plus when someone falls ill or is injured. This offers the employee a way to keep in touch with what is going on, to continue to contribute, and to feel as if they are doing something to move themselves and their team forward. While offering the opportunity to work remotely has been embraced by many employers, there is still a large number who don't trust their people to be working if they're not in the office. After all, you don't know if your employee is in their home office or at the nearest Starbucks.

This seemed to be the case for Emily. Emily's team knew she had to take some downtime to recover. However, they treated her in such a way she felt like they were closing her off from the team. It felt as if they couldn't trust her when she wasn't in their sight. Perhaps they thought she was sitting at home eating bonbons when she should be working. Regardless, they certainly didn't understand that being at home and injured is not actually something that productive, formerly engaged employees, like Emily, want. They would far rather be working with their teams, collaborating, creating, and innovating than at home hurt and feeling unsupported.

For employees like Emily who are injured or ill and have teams that don't believe them, working from home isn't a vacation. It's more like a culling from the herd. When people are injured or ill, they are already feeling vulnerable. To ostracize them at that point is unkind. What they really need from the company is compassion and flexibility.

Compassion at work is often pushed aside by time pressure, workload, financial worries, and other business concerns that take precedence over human concerns. However, research shows us compassion has business value. Compassion as part of an organization's values makes a measurable, positive difference in productivity, financial performance, profitability, and enhanced customer retention. Further, studies show when compassion is part of a business unit's values, as rated by members of the unit, executives deem those units as more effective, they have better financial performance, and realize higher employee and customer retention.[2]

Empathy belongs on every leader's roadmap. Empathy is defined as the ability to understand and share the feelings of another. If you can truly understand how someone else feels, it's easy to display compassion for them. When an employee is hurting, and their illness or injury could, potentially, harm corporate capabilities like creativity and efficiency, empathy restores, and even strengthens, the ability of the organization to accomplish its goals.[3] When empathy is part of the company culture, employees come together to support those who are ill or injured. They will band together to pick up the extra workload and keep things running until their colleague can return to work.

In a supportive culture of compassion and empathy, employees who have to take time away from the job still feel like valued members of the team. They feel safe that they're still wanted by the company. It's not only those employees who are affected by this. The employees who are still working are very aware of how the sick or injured employee is being treated. They come to know this is the way the workplace operates, and they know this is how they will be treated if they ever have bad fortune befall them.

Companies generally refer to their workforce as a "team" that works together for the general good. But just as a company can build up that sense, it can also tear it down. When something bad happens to one of their employees, managers have the power to influence how the other members of their team will react to the situation. An empathetic manager will encourage the team to stay in contact with the injured employee, making them feel part of the day-to-day, even if they're not there physically. Further, the team will feel they can't turn away from someone who is in a difficult state. After all, it may be they will need the team's support some day themselves. However, if the manager does not have that sense of compassion, the team will be aware of it, and will assume that is the way they, too, should behave.

So, how can managers awaken this sense of empathy in themselves, their teams, and their organizations?

First, leaders should understand their power as a role model for behaviour. Leaders guide others throughout organizations in how to think, feel, and act when something happens to a member of their team, simply through how they behave. Recall the situation presented earlier in the chapter when

I described the reaction to my taking time off to recover from the flu. The manager clearly communicated what she actually felt, versus what she had said days earlier. Her actions were contrary to what she had said, and carried much more weight. It was apparent to her entire team that they were not to take any time off, no matter how ill they were.

If we study the theories of transformational leadership, we find this process is one where "leaders and followers raise one another to higher levels of morality and motivation."[4] Leaders first create change by changing themselves, then others emulate their actions, permeating change throughout the team. Therefore, if leaders want to encourage empathy on their teams, they must display empathy themselves. If they model behaviour that doesn't display empathy, it's their behaviour that sends the clearest message, and is what their team members will ultimately emulate.

When managers take the time to develop a relationship with their team members, they are far more likely to feel empathy when something bad happens. After all, they now know this person not just as a worker, but as a human. Further, if they've taken the time to learn what makes their team members tick—what drives them to do great work, what makes them come to work each day, what spurs on their productivity—then it'll be hard for them to imagine that same productive team member faking injury or prolonging illness just to get out of work.

Jeff Weiner, CEO of LinkedIn, is one of the ten most liked CEOs in America.[5] Perhaps it's because of his well-publicized principle of managing compassionately. Here is what he wrote:

> "Of all the management principles I have adopted over the years, either through direct experience or learning from others, there is one I aspire to live by more than any other. I say "aspire" because as much as I'd like to do it consistently and without fail, given the natural ebb and flow of day-to-day operations and challenges, and the subsequent range of responses that follow, I find this particular principle harder to practice consistently than others. That principle is managing compassionately."[6]

Although he mentions it's not always easy to lead in this way, Mr. Weiner clearly wants this to be something that he does. As such, it has become a cultural norm at LinkedIn. It's true—it's not always easy to display empathy. Tasks, deadlines, schedules, deliverables, projects, and pressure continue to mount, regardless of what is happening in our personal lives. It is in circumstances exactly like these that leaders must take a minute to determine why the other person has reached the conclusion they have. What has happened to make them behave a certain way? Or what have they learned that makes them think a certain way? If we can fully grasp that (or even partially, but *try* to feel what they feel), we can take an otherwise challenging situation and turn it into a collaborative experience that raises everyone up.

If you want to develop your empathy skills, try building these tips into your plan:

- Listen, really listen, to what your team members have to say. We talked at length about this in the last chapter. It's by listening that you learn about your employee—what makes them engaged and what keeps them up at night. You'll learn how important their work is and, in the process, you'll come to trust they have the best intentions at heart. Had Emily's second manager take the time to get to know her, he would have understood the pride she took in her work and her desire to be productive, in spite of her injury.

- Be cognizant of your attitude. Do you have an open mind? Are you ready to listen?

- Pay attention to what they say, to their tone of voice, and to their body language. Your people will tell you what you need to know to support them and to help them through challenging times. Many people think they're listening, but what they're actually doing is waiting for their chance to speak and give advice. That's not listening. Take in all they're telling you and consider it carefully. You might find your presumptions are challenged, and you might change your tune.

- If you can't determine, with all that listening, what the team member wants and needs, why not ask? Have them explain their position. This approach is simple, direct, and can be very effective.

People generally start off as empathetic. Look at children—they display empathy in play with other children all the time. For some reason it starts to wear off, though, as people grow into adulthood. The traditional, cut-throat business world certainly doesn't embrace the concept of empathy. But that's changing. Workplaces now put focus on company culture and making their business environments someplace people will want to go to every day. However, it seems they are missing the mark somewhat, because people are still feeling disconnected from their companies and their managers. It seems empathy is more talked about than practiced.

## Encouraging empathy in yourself, your team, and your company

To be empathic, a manager has to look beyond their "world" and individual concerns to see the big workplace picture. After so much time spent looking at the tasks, deadlines, and projects before them though, this outward approach can be difficult. The good news is empathy skills can be improved with some practice. The next time you speak with someone, take some time to ask about their experiences and what they think and feel (this doesn't have to be done at work—you can practice on just about anyone you meet). Displaying some interest in others is a good way to get them talking. When they do open up, be sure to follow the tips above for a more empathic conversation.

When you take the time to understand others, they will feel more inclined to share with you, and maybe even trust you. Certainly, they will feel more like they are partnering in the team's success with you. Also, you may find that you like them! Imagine what that can do to create a supportive and productive workplace atmosphere. In the previous chapter, I provided a rationale for having one on one conversations with the members of your team. Empathy can be a big part of these conversations, so allow that to be part of the plan. Many of the questions provided as conversation jumping-off points will lead to an empathy-based discussion.

As mentioned before, managers' behaviour serves as a powerful model for the members of their teams to use as reference. If a manager is displaying empathy and creating the kind of workplace that encourages caring and compassion, it won't be long before the people who work for them will follow suit. This becomes the new workplace culture. Since it is a kinder, more welcoming culture, it's easier for people to embrace it and grow within it. Remember, the idea of transformational leadership tells us leaders can create change by first changing themselves. Their actions speak to the behaviour that their team members will emulate. By displaying an attitude of empathy, managers will encourage that same attitude in those they work with.

What about the organization? How can managers change the view toward empathy in their companies?

When business units operate from a position of empathy, they perform better. Senior leadership notices those units performing better financially, and that they retain more customers. Furthermore, employees on those teams are more likely to stay within that empathic culture, resulting in lower costs from absenteeism, burnout, or turnover. It's hard to argue with success, so leaders will look to those units and examine the secrets to their success. They may even turn this into a model for the organization.

## Some questions to ask about empathy in a one on one:

- What can I do to help you?
- What can the company do to help you?
- What is one thing you wish I knew about you but don't?
- Has anyone on the team connected with you?
- Does anyone on the team help you?

# SUPPORT

When you spend a large part of your life working with a company, department, and team, you hope they will understand you, believe in you, and support you in your efforts. When that doesn't happen, it feels like a betrayal.

In *Start with Why*, Simon Sinek tells us we are drawn to leaders and organizations who are good at communicating what they believe. They draw us in with their ability to make us feel special, like we belong, and are safe and supported by others, and that inspires us to do great work. If the leader is great, they will earn our loyalty by creating a strong bond with us.[1] However, the opposite will hold true if the leader isn't so great. We will in time feel a sense of discord—almost betrayal—because things are so different from what we had hoped.

Managers hold a position of power and influence, and we follow them because we want to. However, we don't have to follow them if they're not doing the job they should. When that happens, we leave them.

This isn't really a surprise. People are looking to their work (and workplace) to fulfill four basic needs:

- Renewal (Physical)
- Value (Emotional)
- Focus (Mental)
- Purpose (Spiritual)

## IT'S NOT THEM, IT'S YOU

A study done by The Energy Project and Harvard Business Review found when employees perceive those four needs are met, they do their best work (30% higher capacity to focus, nearly 50% greater level of engagement—which we already know drastically affects productivity). To add to that, there is a 63% higher likelihood employees will stay with the company.[2]

Let's focus on only one of these areas—value. When employees feel valued, appreciated, and supported at work, they'll feel more secure, and as a result will have a deeper level of trust. They'll feel far less like they have to defend their position and will have the freedom to create good work.

To explore this way of thinking further, we can surmise that supported employees also have a feeling of higher purpose. They feel what they do matters and serves the company. This is a powerful source of motivation.

These four factors point to our major theme—respect. We'll go into that further later in the book. For now, we'll look at what happens to performance when people don't feel supported and respected. After being treated badly, employee performance plummets. Merely witnessing this bad treatment will cause others' productivity to reduce by almost 50%. Uncivil behaviour on the part of managers nearly always has negative results. Employees are less creative, and many walk out. Approximately 50% will decrease their efforts or lower the quality of their work.[3]

We saw evidence of this with Simone. The mistreatment she received from her manager caused her to feel intimidated and worried. Her work suffered as she second-guessed everything she did. She was unwilling to take any risks at all, and constantly checked and re-checked her work so as not to be punished for anything that may not have been done perfectly.

We also saw evidence of this in Tom's story. Tom was bullied and harassed. He was called out in front of clients and coworkers. It's very clear his manager didn't support him. You couldn't blame Tom had he been less productive. It's a testament to his character that he continued to produce quality material. This was done for the benefit of the client and to protect Tom's reputation, and not for the company. Coworkers who witnessed the lack of support Tom received and how he handled his treatment with integrity and professionalism sided with Tom. Some made the decision to decrease their efforts, still others made the decision to leave, and encouraged Tom to do the same.

## Leaders need to support their people and be a model for others

As we learned in the previous chapter, leaders have a powerful influence on the behaviour of those who work for them. This can mean employees align themselves with their leader's way of thinking or, as we see in this chapter, with those who are not aligned or supported.

Leaders should be modelling supportive behaviour and civility. They need to be aware of this in others and, most importantly, in themselves. Any employee who treats others badly, who bullies and harasses others, and who treats coworkers with disrespect should be called out on this behaviour and given training and the opportunity to change. This includes managers. Just because someone is in a position of power over others does not give them permission to treat people with a lack of respect. This sort of behaviour must be dealt with quickly and with clear expectations of what has to change. There should also be consequences for both employees and managers if the behaviour doesn't change accordingly.

It's highly unlikely these managers left business school thinking "when I have a team, I'm going to be disrespectful and unsupportive." What's far more likely is they've felt the anxiety, pressure, and stress of a busy workplace, and have found themselves unprepared to deal with it. As a result, they respond in dysfunctional ways. Managers need to have self-knowledge in order to be engaging leaders.

## Developing self-awareness

How can you develop self-awareness? Here are some ideas:[4]

- Start by taking a personality test. There are lots of these types of assessments available online. Some of the best known are Myers-Briggs and StrengthsFinder, but there are others available. Perhaps your workplace utilizes one of them and you can leverage that one. Most of these tests work in a similar fashion, highlighting your strengths and how you can maximize that in your work. On the flip side, they also point out some of the things you need to work on developing. Once you've completed your test and considered the results, you may find yourself taking a different approach to your work and your relationships with others.

- If you'd like to gather some very clear feedback about your management style, consider doing a 360-degree assessment, which includes requesting feedback from the people you work with. When carrying out this type of evaluation, you'll want to include your boss, your team members, and peers from other departments. Without feedback, it's difficult for anyone to know how well they're performing. 360-degree feedback helps us to understand the perceptions of those we work with and the impact we have on their success.

- Ask for regular informal feedback. In the chapter on relationships, gathering feedback from your team members was listed as something you can include in your one on one sessions. Why not ask your people how they view your support when discussing professional development?

- Ask for feedback and coaching from your manager. Have you scheduled regular one on one conversations with them? If not, perhaps you should ask for it.

- Do some personal reflection. Take time to examine the way you work and interact with others on your team. You'll need quiet time for this. Why not take a few moments at the end of each work day to reflect on what happened throughout that day—the good, the bad, and yes, even the ugly? Or try reflecting on the previous day's interactions while drinking your morning coffee. I find I get my best thinking done when I'm walking the dogs early in the morning before work. Regardless of when you do your deep thinking, be sure to channel your thinking in a productive manner. Write down your reflections and ideas. You can use a journal, or even jot ideas down in your planner. Of course, you can do this on your computer, but I find it deeply satisfying to write these things down in my planner (yep–I still write stuff down in an old-school planner) or on post-its I put up on the wall. Regardless of the method you use for taking notes, be sure to follow up on what you've decided for yourself. The idea of reflecting and taking notes is to make positive changes for better results. Great thoughts aren't worth much until they're put into action.

- Seek out a mentor or coach to help you grow. A good coach will ask you challenging questions, hold you accountable to your desired changes, and get you to *really* consider your thoughts and actions. A mentor will offer their experience for you to learn and benefit from.

- Be kind to yourself, and model self-care. Your people need you to support them, and you can't do that when you're not feeling your best. Set an example of taking care of yourself by exercising, eating well, and getting plenty of rest. In 2018, Sleep Country Canada put out a funny ad with the message of how bad sleep affects all of us. In the ad, they highlighted how people who don't get enough sleep make bad decisions, carry out tasks poorly, and are cranky.[5] The clear message is we can't be at our best if we're tired and grouchy. As a manager, you can't properly support and care for your team members if you're not at your best.

Below are some questions leaders should ask themselves when developing their self-awareness: [6]

1. What are your core values? How do they impact the way you manage others? How do they impact your expectations of work?

2. What are your dominant personality traits, and how do they impact how you work with others?

3. What aspects of your personality have caused you to behave in destructive ways in the past, especially when you were anxious or overwhelmed?

4. How do you cope with stress at work? What techniques or strategies do you employ? Are you a good role model for your team when dealing with stress?

In reality, most bad managers are actually pretty good people that choose bad responses to the pressures they're facing. By having self-knowledge of how they behave in pressure-filled situations, good managers can keep themselves from behaving badly. When this happens, they're modelling the type of behaviour that engages people in a good way. That's what they truly want their team members to emulate.

## To get the most from your people, give them what they want.

In his book *What People Want: A Manager's Guide to Building Trust-based Relationships with Your People*, author and workplace consultant and coach Terry Bacon tells us the top three needs of five hundred employees surveyed were: honesty, fairness, and trust. In the paragraphs below, we will explore those further:[7]

> Honesty–People want to feel they can be honest with others, and that those people will be honest with them. This includes their managers. It doesn't mean managers can deliver the truth any way they want. For example, if under the guise of talking straight, a manager delivers the truth in a brutal fashion, their employee will understandably not take it well. Straight talk is important to establishing trust, but it must be delivered with tact, skill, and good judgment.[8] Consider how Simone felt when she was told her manager never wanted her on his team. That's got to hurt.
>
> Fairness–People want to be appreciated for their accomplishments. They want to feel pride in what they do, and feel acknowledged for

what they contribute. They want to feel relevant and that they're contributing to something they believe in. They don't want to feel as if they're irrelevant or being treated as second-class employees.

Trust–Trust is a fundamental relationship requirement. Without it, there is no relationship. Employees need to feel that their manager trusts them to produce good work, and they need to be able to trust that their managers are leading with integrity.

The author also goes on to list a number of managerial "don'ts", including these thoughts which are directly related to providing support:

- Don't bully people intellectually (and I will add, don't bully people at all)
- Don't be condescending
- Don't minimize the contributions of others
- Don't attack the person rather than the problem
- Don't use threats

In the case of both Simone and Tom, these "don'ts" were definitely done. We saw examples of how this behaviour crept into the relationships with their managers, and how it affected the work and sense of security that both Simone and Tom expected in the workplace. Further, we saw how the behaviour displayed by the managers also affected others on the team who witnessed the bad behaviour, and changed their work patterns or even quit as a result.

What employees really need from their manager is a feeling of support, trust, and security in order to do their best work.

## What if you just don't like them?

Sometimes people don't mesh well with one another. If it's a performance issue, coaching, training, and consistent support—along with a great attitude and effort from the employee—can help the situation. But what if it's interpersonal? It seems there is little that can be done about that.

Well, perhaps there are some things that can be done.

Firstly, understand that you don't actually have to like someone to be able to work effectively with them. Of course, it's nice if you do, but you can still recognize and appreciate their skills, abilities, and knowledge without being friends. If you dislike an employee, you have to be very aware of how you're treating them so as not to unconsciously treat them unfairly.[9]

Secondly, respect what they bring to your team. People who you like often display the same characteristics that you possess, so it's easy to recognize their contributions. That's great for getting along, but it's not necessarily the best for propelling the group to success. People who are different from you—who have different ways of perceiving things—will challenge the way things are done, and present new and fresh points of view.

Learning how to handle your frustration will help you to control your reactions. We've looked at some ways to develop your self-awareness. Now that you're aware of how you think and feel, become aware of how you react when in challenging situations. Remember, the employee you don't really care for didn't install the buttons they're pushing. They found them by accident.

As a manager, it's your job to be fair, impartial, and to work well with all of your employees. To fully support your reports in their work, you must set aside your feelings for the employee and be professional and positive.

If you develop a regular cadence for one on one conversations with the employee in question, you might find that you can actually uncover things you have in common. Set your mind to seeking out their positive traits; everyone has something good to offer. Keep that in mind as you work with them, and over time you might even find that you come to appreciate them.

Regardless of whether there ever comes a time when you like this person, be sure to support and evaluate them fairly. If you're aware of your bias, you can take steps to work around it during review periods or feedback sessions. Ask yourself, "Am I using the same standards I would use for other people?" You can also ask others who work with the employee for their feedback. It could be there are positive contributions that were overlooked.

## To sum it up…

In this book, we've quoted the Gallup survey on employee engagement several times, because it covers what employees *want* in order to engage them and keep them engaged. Here is a summary of what they want from their managers:[10]

- Help in keeping them focused
- Knowing them
- Caring about them
- Hearing them
- Helping them to feel proud of what they've accomplished
- Helping them to see their value
- Giving them access to the tools and resources they need to do good work
- Challenging them to do great work
- Helping them to see the importance of their contribution to the company and to the team

In other words, giving them support.

## Some questions to ask about providing support in a one on one:

- Are you happy working here?

- Is there anyone on the team whom you find difficult to work with? Why is that?

- How can I help you?

- What is frustrating you right now?

- Would you like coaching? With what?

- How do you think we could work better together?

# PROMOTION

If you're a manager with a high-performing team that gets along and does great work, it's understandable you'd want everything to remain just as it is, forever. It's so satisfying. Looking out at your group of employees, happily working together and being productive, is enough to warm any manager's heart. Indeed, this is also enough to warm the hearts of the employees, who genuinely enjoy working in this type of environment.

In business life (or regular life) staying that warm and fuzzy way forever just doesn't happen. Change always creeps in and disrupts everything. Those same employees who are happily working and being productive start to have thoughts of bigger and better things.

You, the manager, may be content to have your team moving along like the well-oiled machine it is, but your people are looking at this productivity and great work performance as their ticket to a higher-level job with all the perks, including a pay raise.

This was the case with Percy, and he didn't try to hide it. On the contrary, he spoke about his plans for his future many times with his manager(s). While managers are in a position to help their employees move up in a company, each employee really is in the driver's seat for their career. It's up to them to take ownership of their career, and Percy certainly did so. His managers backed him up in these future-focused conversations, often telling him he was senior management and eventually executive material, and that they would help him get on a path to these roles. Understandably, Percy became frustrated and disillusioned when conversation after conversation about his career resulted in no forward progression.

Percy wasn't actually with the company that long; his tenure was only a couple of years. However, during that time Percy saw many others elevated to higher-level roles. When that happened, it made sense that Percy would want—maybe even expect—the same thing to happen for him. To add fuel to the fire, in his point of view, his managers had made what amounted to a promise to get him into one of the high-level management roles. It was clear that the company didn't have a requirement for someone to be in a role for a certain length of time before getting a promotion, so he didn't know why they were holding him back.

Helping employees develop their skills and move forward in their careers is an important part of being a manager, yet this is an area most managers neglect. The price of neglect is a high one, because those employees who hunger for something more will go after it, even if it means going to another company.

Millennials now form the largest generation in the US, so it makes sense we would look at their trends to deduce what will happen in the workplace. In Gallup's report "How Millennials Want to Work and Live,"[1] we learn that millennials are the least engaged generation in the workforce. Only 29% of millennials are engaged, meaning that most workers really don't feel connected to their jobs or workplaces. They may start out in a job with all kinds of passion and energy, but they quickly check out when their needs aren't recognized.

This group isn't really formed from a bunch of non-committed job-hoppers, as popular opinion would have you believe. They don't want to switch jobs, but their companies aren't giving them a reason to stay. They're looking for opportunities, and would actually love for those opportunities to come from their current employers. However, if opportunities don't materialize, millennials are more prone to look elsewhere for something better. Studies show that 60% of millennials are open to new job opportunities. This is significantly higher than non-millennial workers. However, even non-millennials are looking for something more. The same studies show that 45% of non-millennial workers are open to something else.

According to Gallup, millennials, and probably others from different generations, are not pursuing job satisfaction, but rather development. It's what drives this generation. In a related study, Gallup also found that most people will look outside the company when they're ready to make a career move. The majority of American adults (93%) say that they left for a new employer the last time they changed roles.[2] Imagine the impact on a company when that happens! There is a great deal of time, effort, and money spent hiring people and getting them to proficiency in their jobs. It's been estimated the cost to replace a high-level employee can equal as much as 150% of the employee's annual salary. All of that investment walks out with them when they change companies. What a waste! More than this, the loss of a key team member has other costs—damage to team dynamics, extra work for team members who have to take on the additional load until a replacement can be brought up to speed, negative impact on workplace culture, and interestingly enough, it can place a drain on a company's leadership pipeline.

Companies often look to hiring outside candidates when new roles open up. It may be this is the best option, but what does it do to the morale of existing employees? Hiring internally leads to greater engagement. Employees see their company will offer them a developmental path and opportunities for the future. Hiring internally has the added benefits of cultural fit and the retention of company lore. It's also the case that people promoted into new roles tend to have a shorter learning curve than those brought in from outside the organization. While it's not always the best solution to promote internally versus hiring from outside, companies and their managers should have a policy of looking inside first.

Smart companies will have succession plans with future leader prospects in mind. We've all heard the coming years will see a great number of people leaving the workforce to retire. There will be a large talent gap to fill, so it makes sense for companies and their managers to look at who the leadership prospects are. This first step was certainly done for Percy, but it was never taken any further. This doesn't make much sense. If companies feel a negative impact on their leadership pipeline, why don't they develop people to fill that pipeline internally?

It's natural for employees to want to learn, grow, and advance in their careers. It's a real shame they feel they have to leave their organizations to make this happen. One big factor in rectifying this is for managers to position their people for growth and greater success.

In the chapter on relationships, we talked about managers getting to know their people—what makes them tick and what drives them forward. If you know your employee well, you as a manager should be providing feedback, demonstrating you care, and taking an interest in their personal goals. As mentioned before, none of this talk will mean anything if the manager doesn't help the employee to put a plan into action. Managers can help employees stay on track with their career goals, and can help the company improve its leadership pipeline by making progression and development a regular part of the one on one conversation. Remember, when employees feel they can talk to their managers, they are far more likely to be engaged in their jobs, and far more likely to stay with their company. If they know they've been heard and that their manager understands their desire to grow, they will be even more likely to stay. Finally, if a manager makes a promise to help the employee with career progression, then that promise must be acted upon. Certainly, the perfect new role may not be available exactly when the employee is ready for it. However, regular conversations about what's likely to happen, along with reassurance that the manager has the employee's interests at heart, will go a long way with improving the employee's patience and happiness on the job while waiting for something to open up. In the meantime, the employee should be challenged by projects, learning opportunities, job shadowing more senior roles, etc.

Employees are looking for a manager they can count on, a job that suits their skills and talents, and growth opportunities. If their manager and company can do this for them, they will likely stay in their job, and continue to grow and develop.

## If development is so important, why don't managers focus on it?

There is always so much going on in any given workplace. People are busy trying to be as productive, innovative, creative, and profitable as they can. They're working hard at doing more with less, dealing with change, and trying to satisfy customers. There's only so much managers can focus on at any given time, so development conversations tend to get lost in the noise as managers focus more on the day-to-day and less on longer-term activities that are less certain and harder to control.[3]

In chaotic times, even one on one conversations tend to focus more on tasks at hand versus employee development. Employees also tend to focus on the issues immediately before them instead of those impacting their future. Then, later, they have a sense of disquiet as they wonder what happened to their plans for career progression within the company. As mentioned before, employees are in control of their careers, and should be keeping this topic top of mind. However, it can all too easily get lost in the task clutter, and is then shuffled to the bottom of the deck. After a while, it can feel as if the talk about career planning was just that—talk.

---
*Not enough time is just an excuse.*

---

All too often managers will simply run out of time before they get to this part of the one on one conversation. But that's not good enough for your team members. Remember, they really want to grow and develop, and would probably prefer to do that with the company they're currently with. It's a lot of work to go outside and find a new job, so it makes sense they would stay where they are if they feel engaged and on a solid development path.

Managers would be wise to show genuine care for their team members' futures. Talented people want to advance, and managers want to keep talented people in the company. So, it stands to reason that managers should devote some time to training, mentoring, and coaching their people. If their current company won't provide that kind of support, we've seen that employees will look for it elsewhere.

Some questions to ask about employee development and promotion in a one on one:

- What do you want to achieve?
- What are your career goals for the next year? Five years?
- How is the work you're doing contributing to the goals?
- How do your goals tie in to the organization's goals?
- Are you passionate about what you're working on?
- Do you think you're ready for more? Why?
- What would you like to learn more about to help you achieve those goals?

# EMPOWERMENT

*It doesn't make sense to hire smart people and
then tell them what to do. We hire smart people
so they can tell us what to do.* —Steve Jobs

The saying goes, "If you want something done right, do it yourself."[1] But is this really the best thing for today's time-strapped managers? If you Google "delegation," more than 26,000,000 entries are returned. Google "empowerment," and you will have more than 257,000,000 returns. It's clear this is a topic of interest, and it's likely that many of those millions of results will be viewed by managers who are seeking strategies to become less busy.

In today's workplace, people are extremely busy. Managers will tell you the number one reason they don't coach or have regular and frequent one on ones is a lack of time. But the very best way to maximize productivity and ensure good results is by drawing on the talents of the people on the team—which are developed when that time is invested.

According to the online Business Dictionary, empowerment is:

- the management practice of sharing information, rewards, and power with employees so they can take initiative and make decisions to solve problems and improve service and performance.

The idea here is for the manager to give employees skills, resources, tools, opportunity, authority, and motivation to independently do the job they know they should do that is best for the customer and the company. Of course, the other side of making these provisions is holding employees responsible for outcomes—making them accountable for the work they do, the decisions they make, and connecting the dots on how this contributes to their goals, performance, and productivity.

The business world has embraced the idea of empowering employees, or at least delegating tasks, as a way of moving things off managers' to-do lists. However, a great many managers find this tough to do. Why is that? It's all about giving up power.

## Giving up power–should you or shouldn't you?

According to Toister, there are a few reasons managers fear the loss of power.[2] Firstly, managers are afraid that allowing employees to make decisions will have costly results. Managers are responsible for the success of their teams and their projects. If they give up some power, it could put that work at risk. They fear there could be a lack of consistency in service delivery or policy adherence, and maybe even in customers' perception of the company. It could also be that managers are not willing to put in the work to train their people to be able to make necessary decisions. It takes a lot of work to create the training and guidelines, and to provide feedback to ensure employees are doing the right thing. All in all, it just seems easier for managers to make all the decisions themselves, rather than invest time and effort in developing employees.

As a result, it might seem the easiest course of action for a manager to take would be to tighten control, rather than loosen it by empowering employees. Research shows, though, that giving employees more autonomy can boost innovation and success.[3] It also shows that clamping down and refusing to empower employees can end up doing a disservice to the company. When managers rule with an iron fist, employees feel excessively pressured, not trusted, and will chafe under the scrutiny.

Some managers may fear the loss of power and influence over their team members. This could happen, but if the team works in an empowered, inclusive way, everyone should be empowered, including the manager. Instead of being diminished, managers in an empowered workplace will find their roles take on greater meaning. Empowered managers have the wherewithal to guide their people to take on greater challenges and achieve greater collective organizational success.

Empowered employees think, take action, and make decisions on their own. It doesn't mean they're not expected to follow the guidelines set out by their managers. Rather, empowerment is about understanding what is best for the department and company, and having permission to make the best decision given the situation.

## Empowering your employees

When managers empower their people, they're simply promoting ownership.[4] Here are some reasons why you, as a manager, should do that:

1. You'll get more done. When workers are empowered to do their jobs, they'll connect with the organization. Empowered employees will want to do their best work because of the connection they feel. When managers trust their people to act in the best interests of the company and make their own decisions, they see results well beyond projected outcomes.

2. You'll improve communication. Empowering people involves communicating with them. It doesn't mean managers are completely hands-off. Rather, empowerment is a result of open and frank communication about the current situation and what should be done. Empowered employees also understand the importance of timely and open communication with their managers.

3. You'll have a positive impact. As we learned in the stories above, people don't work just to collect a paycheck. They work to feel they've contributed, and to feel valued. Empowerment leads to greater initiative, motivation, workplace satisfaction, and commitment.

4. You'll like it! By helping others grow, develop, and do great work, managers can enjoy a real sense of satisfaction. After all, they're part of something great, and that's a pretty cool feeling. Empowered

employees appreciate the trust and support coming from their bosses, and they offer their loyalty and best work in return.

Looking back on Elton's story, we can see how the manager's removing all empowerment from his employees resulted in people leaving the team. We examined the effect on the employee. But what about the manager?

By removing all decision-making approval from his team members, Elton's manager put himself in the position of needing to check over every detail. In his interview with me, Elton mentioned there were times when he was not allowed to send emails without cc-ing his manager or running those communiques past him first for approval. Imagine the time added to each little task because of that! Now remember how time-strapped most managers are, and you can certainly see why adding delays of this kind ultimately takes a toll on a manager's productivity.

Even the worst micromanagers will tell you they dream of having a team that can operate independently. They love the idea of employees taking initiative, showing they understand what is important to the company and the department, and being super-productive. But they sabotage these dreams by micromanaging and thereby get in the way of that independence. It's likely this isn't because the manager wants to be considered selfish or autocratic. Rather, it's likely they just haven't taken the time to focus on creating an environment of empowerment.

## How does one create an environment of empowerment?[5]

- Take advantage of opportunities given by conducting one on ones. The communication and relationship-building that happens during one on ones leads to better relationships and more trust. It's much easier for the manager to let go and empower employees when they are familiar with the employees' work and ways of thinking. One on ones also create the opportunity for managers to communicate what's happening in the company, provide the opportunity to ask questions, and ensure employees understand what is important for peak productivity.

- Provide plenty of information. Most leaders carry a lot of knowledge around with them. The challenge is they don't always share what they know, and then they expect their team members to be able to make good decisions and take action as if they had insider knowledge. In order to be fair, managers should make a habit of taking what is important for their people to know and sharing it in a structured and consistent manner. If employees clearly understand the what and the why behind goals and tasks, they can make better decisions and take appropriate action in any situation.

- Clearly define roles. If employees don't know what they're supposed to be doing, then how can they be expected to do it well? They need to know their boundaries—who is doing what, and at what point they may be stepping on the toes of others. By establishing specific roles and responsibilities, employees can all work together cooperatively and are clear on what to do.

- Create accountability. Empowered employees also need to know what's expected of them, when they've met or exceeded expectations, and when they haven't. To motivate them to always do their best, be sure to regularly follow up on their progress, reward them when they're doing well, and offer support if they're falling off the rails.

- Encourage independence. Constantly looking over team members' shoulders is not only annoying (for them and for the manager), but is also a waste of time. Give people the chance to stretch and make their own decisions. They may stumble, but they will learn in the process and ultimately be stronger and better employees.

- Celebrate success. Empowered people want to feel their leader appreciates what they do. Find ways to acknowledge their contributions, thank them for their efforts, and celebrate what they've done well.

- Redirect if necessary. In *The New One Minute Manager*, Ken Blanchard and Spencer Johnson suggest using the "One Minute

Redirect" if things are going off-track. In a One-Minute Redirect, the manager specifies exactly what went wrong and makes sure the original goal is clear. If the original goal isn't clear, then steps are taken to clarify it and the manager takes responsibility. Once the facts are confirmed, the manager explains how they feel about the mistake, what the impact was on results, and then reminds the employee they are better than the mistake, and that they are confident it will not be repeated. The redirect ends with the manager reaffirming the employee's value to the team and the manager's full support in getting them back on track. Since it ends in a supportive way, the employee still feels empowered to carry on, rather than belittled and punished.[6]

---

*People who feel good about themselves produce good results*
—Ken Blanchard and Spencer Johnson

---

There's always a balance in empowering your employees. Managers must learn what they should control, and what they can turn over to their people. In empowering their people, managers reduce frustration and enhance job satisfaction. They help their people to feel more like partners in the success of the business instead of minions who are there to do the company's bidding.

## Some questions to ask about empowerment in a one on one:

- How do you prefer to work?
- What do you do when you get stuck on something?
- How can I help?
- How do your goals tie in to the organization's goals?

- How is the work you're doing contributing to those goals?
- What do you want to achieve?

# CONSIDERATION

Being considerate is one of those virtues that doesn't show up very often in management textbooks. Likely, that's because it's not so much a management skill as it is a life skill.

One of the recurring themes of this book is that people are more likely to put in their best efforts for you when you act positively toward them. This includes being considerate. Each employee is an important part of the business, and the human family, and should be treated as such. It's the Golden Rule in action, and it's recognized in nearly every culture and religion worldwide. In *The Speed of Trust*, Stephen M.R. Covey itemizes some examples of this:[1]

- Christianity: "*Do unto others as you would have them do unto you.*"

- Judaism: "*What you hate, do not do to anyone.*"

- Islam: "*No one of you is a believer until he loves for his brother what he loves for himself.*"

- Buddhism: "*Hurt not others with that which pains thyself.*"

- Confucianism: "*What you do not want done to yourself, do not do to others.*"

Considerate people understand that the feelings, ideas, and actions of others have meaning—even if only to them. As a result, they take time to understand the people they work with. They get to know what their goals are, what drives them, and what they value. They look at the work that has been done and consider the effort that has gone into it—even if the results are not what was hoped for.

It's likely no surprise that the secret to finding out what's important to employees is to ask them questions and develop relationships in the one on one. It's amazing how that simple practice supports the idea of consideration. After all, it's difficult for a manager to disregard the feelings and ideas of people when they've gotten to know them.

Considerate managers ask thoughtful questions designed to get employees engaged in the conversation. They don't ask questions to make others feel uncomfortable or afraid. When responses are given, considerate managers will listen carefully, and think before making a response. In *The Seven Habits of Highly Effective People*, Stephen R. Covey puts forward the notion of "*Seek first to understand*" (Habit 5).[2] Seeking first to understand involves a paradigm shift wherein managers will listen with the intent to understand their team member before replying. Most people listen with the intent to speak. That is to say, they listen with their own filters firmly in place, e.g., what does this mean to me? How am I affected? They're listening, but are formulating their replies at the same time. The net result is they don't really capture what's important to the other person. Seeking first to understand is critical for completely understanding issues and finding the correct outcome.

If one has really listened with the intent to understand, they can then shape their own thoughts in such a way they will resonate with others. They'll appreciate what work *means* to their team members. A manager can't discredit work accomplished if they understand the thoughts and actions that went into it. Considerate managers show their appreciation when team members do good work. When they do, it results in a positive feedback loop that makes all parties involved feel good about the accomplishment. When employees feel their work is recognized and understood, they're more likely to repeat the same amount of effort. Considerate managers also show their understanding of effort and ownership put forth even when projects don't have the best results. They offer feedback and support to address issues and resolve challenges. They appreciate the fact their people did not set out with the intent to fail, and provide the opportunity to rectify wrongs.

Caitlin, in her story, put forward examples of her manager showing favouritism toward some team members and leaving others completely out of the loop. If you're the favoured employee, this can feel nice in the short term, but it becomes uncomfortable overall when others are continually passed over and seemingly ignored. If a manager chooses to be considerate, then they will ensure everyone is engaged in the work as much as possible. Individual efforts will be appreciated, and everyone will be clear on what they bring to the team. This doesn't mean that a manager can't put one employee in charge of others. It simply means when decisions are made, being considerate involves advising the other team members of why this has been decided and how it benefits everyone.

Feedback is very important to everyone. Employees want to know if they're doing well, or if they're starting to veer off the rails. Providing feedback in a considerate fashion means it's delivered candidly, but in a way that demonstrates caring. When giving feedback, look at what happened, why things went well (or not), and what should be changed or repeated going forward. When done positively, this kind of feedback strengthens relationships and leaves people feeling energized and focused on doing great things. Harshly criticizing people, as in the case with Tom's manager, leads to employee's embarrassment and frustration. Publicly berating employees makes things even worse. Who would want to stick around for that kind of humiliation? Blowing things out of proportion also seems less than considerate. In Tom's case, we learned the manager was convinced project deliverables were substandard. However, the client was happy with the results. It seemed the punishment was unreasonable, if not completely unwarranted. When this happens, employees are left wondering what they did wrong. Making small things into a big deal makes a manager look erratic and nitpicky. And, when feedback is delivered in a harsh and mean fashion, it doesn't motivate people to do anything but head for the door.

Managers, your teams need to know they can rely on you! They need to believe you will listen to them, understand them, and treat them with consideration.

In the story shared by Caitlin, we saw that she took initiative to learn about the store's customers and what they needed. She also took the opportunity to explore the internet looking for information on the products carried by the store. Imagine what this means to a manager! Most employees want to be trained and look to the company to provide what they need. In Caitlin's case, she took the bull by the horns and learned what she needed to know to be good at what she did. This should be celebrated by a manager. But Caitlin didn't feel her skill and knowledge was valued. If the manager was truly aware, she would have realized that, of all the staff she had hired over the years, few (if any) other than Caitlin had taken any time on this kind of initiative. It's funny—Caitlin showed a great deal of consideration for the business, the owner, and the customers in educating herself. It would make sense that the owner/manager would return the favour and consider that Caitlin faced customer questions and needs, and had taken steps to provide the knowledge that would help Caitlin feel solid in her job. As Caitlin tells us, there was very little training provided to the staff. They learned how to run the POS system and inventory, but not much else. When appropriate training is not provided, the end result is customers don't get the information they need, and employees feel unsupported.

In decades past, it was believed that people owed a company loyalty simply because they were employed there. Employees used to stay with organizations for many years—often their entire careers—because they felt that was what they had to do. Over time, they amassed knowledge that was specialized to that industry, and that company. As a result, it made sense for them to stay in their lane at that company. But this idea of employee loyalty is changing. A quick search on the internet can tell an employee about any number of other jobs they could do at a variety of other companies. If organizations don't display any kind of consideration for employees beyond a paycheck, employees will understandably strive to work somewhere else where they will potentially have better opportunities and working conditions. Employee loyalty is increasingly hard to find these days. Maybe it's because many companies don't display any kind of loyalty to their employees.

Why worry about loyalty? Loyal employees are committed to the organization and bring their best efforts to the job. The organization, in turn, can better realize its goals and aspirations. Loyal employees display the values and ethics that organizations seek and should want to retain. Caitlin was an employee that displayed this kind of loyalty. Employee loyalty can be defined as an attachment which develops into an emotional attitude toward an organization. The more satisfied an employee is with their workplace, the more loyalty they feel. However, engagement surveys tell us that overall, loyalty is currently pretty low. When one in three employees plans to leave their workplace in the next year, it's obvious loyalty doesn't exist for them. In Caitlin's story we learned the store hired a lot of part-time and full-time employees only to have them leave not long after. Caitlin displayed loyalty and longevity, so it's right to think she should have been more valued. Unfortunately, she didn't feel that way. As new people came in and were touted, by the owner, as the new wonderful thing, Caitlin felt like her contributions didn't count, and became resentful.

Loyalty in the workplace should be reciprocal—an employee's loyalty to a company is contingent on the company's loyalty to them.[3] Therefore, it makes sense for a manager to display loyalty to their team members by having their backs, advocating for them, and valuing their work. The payoff is loyal employees who, as we've learned, will put forward their best efforts to be much more productive in helping the organization achieve its goals.

These days, unfortunately, employees are often seen as short-term resources. Perhaps it's because statistics tell us the average employee tenure is only 4.2 years.[4] In retail, tenure is even a shorter length of time. Is that a reason to give up on good employees, though? That doesn't make sense. What does make sense is for companies to simply be considerate and think about the following:

- What does a new employee need to be successful on the job? Think about their first day, week, month, and quarter. A little investment at the front end can have big payoff later. Considerate managers will take the time to ensure onboarding success.

- Outline your expectations for all your reports. Tenured employees also need to be clear on manager expectations so they, too, can be successful in their work. Often rules and priorities change in the business environment, and considerate managers take the time to explain the "what" and "why" so their people understand how to adapt to changing business environments.

- Consider how the goals and objectives of the organization are communicated to the employee. If they're not communicated, how can employees be expected to work toward them? During one on one discussions, be sure to bring up organizational goals and discuss how the employee's individual work contributes to those goals. Considerate managers realize this isn't something employees will automatically know.

- Ensure all team members are treated as individuals, and consider how they are made to feel at work. This one is easy—refer to the top of the chapter and follow the golden rule. Considerate managers treat others as they would like to be treated.

- Pay attention and engage with those who have been with a company for a while. If they are left to their own devices with little to no feedback, they will start to feel unappreciated. Considerate managers show appreciation for everyone who works on their teams, not just the new people.

- Think before you communicate. Poorly thought-out remarks can alienate, and even insult, team members. Considerate managers think about the message and its impact on their team members before they speak.

- While on that subject ... communicate! Frequent and regular conversations with team members keeps them engaged and in the loop. Considerate managers don't assume information flows equally to everyone.

- Value team members and the work they contribute. When employees feel they've added value and positively impacted the success of the organization, they are, understandably, proud of what they've accomplished. Managers who disregard or undo the work of their team members with no reasoning leave them feeling hurt and maybe even insulted. A simple explanation of what was done well and what could be improved upon can address that upset (again—feedback is so important!). Considerate managers communicate when the outcome is positive and when and why improvements are necessary.

## Some questions to ask about consideration in a one on one:

- How are you?
- What can I do to help you?
- Are you struggling with anything? Can I help?
- Do you have what you need to be successful?
- What can our company/department/team do better?
- What are you finding frustrating right now?

# TRUST

This book is written from the point of view of the employee, and an employee should be able to trust the company and the manager they work for.

When employees trust the organization they work for, they gain confidence. They know their company and their boss have their back, so they're prepared to do good work for them. However, if trust is broken, or never existed in the first place, then suspicion takes its place.[1]

People want to be trusted. If a manager wants to build a strong team, they need to be good at establishing trust by relating to and working well with others, and achieving great results in the process. But, how do you do that? It takes a combination of character (integrity, motives, intentions) and competence (capabilities, skills, results, and track record).[2]

While character is highly important, an employee won't fully trust a manager if they don't think they're capable of getting results. Similarly, a manager may be very good at what they do, but they won't be trusted if they're not honest and don't act with integrity and soundness of character.

According to Dictionary.com, integrity is the "adherence to moral and ethical principle, soundness of moral character, honesty." When someone displays these characteristics, they create a foundation on which trust is built. This is something that every employer is looking for when they hire a new employee. However, trust is not very high at the beginning, which is why companies do such things as reference and background checks. Over time, employers learn how their new hire operates and how they adhere to the moral principles that define integrity. What a manager may not realize is their employees, even the new ones, are looking for the same adherence to principles from them. When their manager walks the talk, those who report to them can begin trusting them.

However, even someone in a position of power can operate with a lack of character. Their demonstrated lack of integrity can make others question their motives and intentions. When this happens, there is no amount of capability that can offset that lack of integrity, and trust will not exist in the relationship. We see this all the time with politicians. They go into elections with the very best of intentions (at least it seems that way) and make all kinds of commitments to the voters. Once in office, though, they often seem to forget about those promises, and appear to abandon the very constituents they vowed to represent. When this happens, it's often the case that they lose their seat come the next election. No amount of power, prestige, or political know-how will guarantee them the voters' trust.

The same holds true for managers. Most employees believe their managers have the know-how and capability to have been given a management role. They put their trust in their managers to know what to do and how to lead. If the managers, however, continually display poor behaviour or a lack of knowledge, their people will begin to wonder how they got their position. What is worse, however, is when the manager demonstrates a lack of character. That's a real trust-breaker.

To illustrate, we'll refer back to Tom's story. Tom worked for a manager who was very good at her job. He believed he was getting top-notch training, and truly wanted to learn more from his boss. He asked repeatedly for project management training (something she was well versed in), but he never received it. Promises were made, but nothing was delivered. We also saw this in Percy's story. He worked for a manager who was highly competent, yet the promises made were never delivered on. He was told over and over that a promotion was in his immediate future, but nothing ever materialized. In both cases, the employees began to doubt what their managers said, and a lack of trust crept in. Actions speak louder than words, so you have to back up your words and take action for trust to exist.

When a team member starts with a new company, they typically do so with the best of intentions. They're excited about their new job and truly want to do good work. An employee is most engaged with a company when they start. At this time, they put their trust in their new employer and expect the employer to uphold the contract providing the promised work environment, benefits programs, office perks, and compensation.

People who work for companies expect to be paid for that work. It's common practice for new employees to sign a contract with their employer outlining the rate of pay, vacation, and benefits policies, etc. Since this contract was offered by the company and signed by officers of that company, employees believe their employers when they say they'll receive a certain amount each payday, and when exactly those paydays are. They further expect there will be money to pay them. Knowing this, it's easy to understand why Tom would have felt upset when his paycheck bounced. In good faith, Tom approached his boss and asked for a replacement check. He was assured this would never happen again, and he believed it. When the next paycheck bounced, his trust was certainly shaken. However, it was the lack of communication, beating around the bush, and posturing over this event that made Tom truly feel betrayed by his employer. This also undermined Tom's sense of safety in the company. Tom's manager, while very competent, did not act with integrity. As a result, Tom lost trust in her and didn't feel secure in his job or at the company.

**HIERARCHY OF NEEDS**

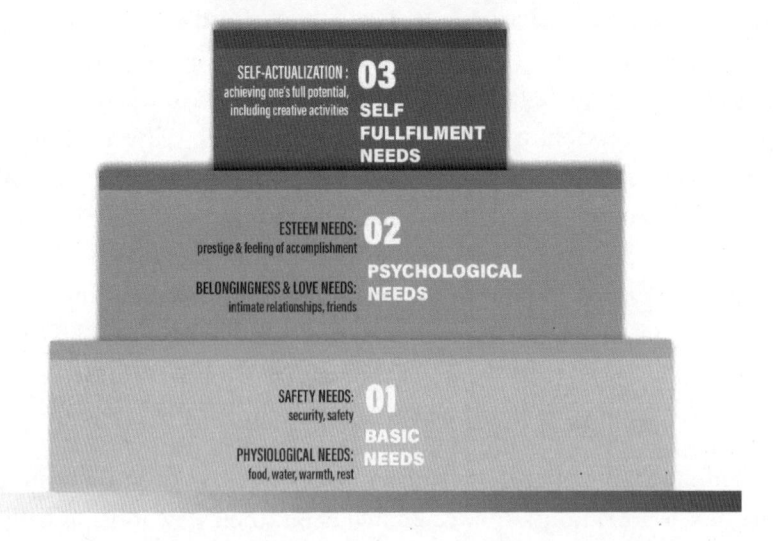

**SELF-ACTUALIZATION: 03**
achieving one's full potential, including creative activities
**SELF FULLFILMENT NEEDS**

**ESTEEM NEEDS: 02**
prestige & feeling of accomplishment
**BELONGINGNESS & LOVE NEEDS:**
intimate relationships, friends
**PSYCHOLOGICAL NEEDS**

**SAFETY NEEDS: 01**
security, safety
**PHYSIOLOGICAL NEEDS:**
food, water, warmth, rest
**BASIC NEEDS**

Maslow's Hierarchy of Needs is a model which classifies human needs. The bottom, and largest, tier is physiological needs, such as food and water, security, and safety. These are the basic needs everyone requires to feel comfortable.

These basic needs must be met before anyone can go on to growing and doing great work.

Making promises that are not kept, not upholding the terms of contracts, and not displaying competence and credibility in work and personal relationships destroy an employee's trust. Trust is most profoundly shaken when basic needs are negatively impacted—the very foundations of a person's needs. In Tom's case, he relied on the promise of a paycheck to make ends meet for his family. When the paychecks bounced, Tom not only felt a lack of security, but he was also concerned with how he would meet the physiological needs of his family, i.e. how he would put food on the table and pay rent. For the safety of his family, Tom was forced to leave his job and find work elsewhere. It goes a little deeper, though. Tom left his job partly because he had to in order to provide for his family, but also because he wanted to. He didn't trust his boss and didn't want to work for someone with that type of character.

When one displays integrity, it should be visible through their words, decisions, and actions. When one does this consistently, they demonstrate they can be trusted. When one does not do this consistently, then the opposite is true. They appear to be, and likely are, untrustworthy.

Percy learned that he couldn't trust the people he reported to. Percy went through a few managers, in just a short amount of time, due to organizational changes. All the managers he ended up with made promises to him. However, none of them upheld those promises. Why do managers do this? Percy took these managers at their word. After all, he was upfront and honest with them about the career track he wanted to be on, and they supported those goals. No one seemed to put up roadblocks or offer any reasons why he shouldn't expect to be supported to go in that direction. If they'd been unable to follow through on that professional development path for Percy, why didn't they just tell him?

The need for respect, or reputation, is also very important to employees. The achievement of this in the workplace is displayed primarily through promotions. The recognition of a title change and upward progression is a major reward for employees. Everyone wants to feel appreciated and recognized. We saw this in Percy's story. That's all he really wanted from his manager—recognition and the commensurate promised reward. Although it may seem a bit shallow to have such a need for accolades and recognition, Percy also felt he needed it to gain respect—both from his colleagues and himself. He desired to move up the hierarchy of needs and achieve his full potential. By stalling him and making false promises, his manager not only appeared to be misleading him, but he also appeared to not care about what was truly important to Percy. As such, this was felt as a betrayal.

Often people think if they bring up a negative topic or something that will come as a disappointment, they'll lose the employee. However, not honouring promises (or ducking the conversation) is what really drove Percy to leave. Making vague promises of promotions and raises might work for the short term. However, over time, employees will begin to see through those false promises. When that happens, the employee-manager relationship is typically damaged beyond repair, and the employee will look for other opportunities.

> *What upsets me is not that you lied to me, but that I can no longer believe you.* —Friedrich Nietzsche

What about the other way around? What if a manager doesn't trust their employees?

## What if you can't trust your team members?

Unfortunately, this happens all the time. Companies recruit people and the first thing they do after interviews is a background and reference check. Once hired, employees are asked to ride out a probation period. The employee has ninety days to prove they can be trusted to do the work. After that, they become part of the performance management process, where they're constantly being judged against certain standards (generally ill-defined) to see whether they measure up well enough to get an annual raise and be trusted to do another year of work. Is this really a good way to establish a productive and engaging working relationship? Having said that, employees do need to have feedback on their performance, which brings us back to (you guessed it) the one on one conversation. It all comes down to this important practice. If managers are having regular conversations with their team members, they'll learn what they do well, what they need a little support with, and what is expected of them. They will also learn the character of each of their team members. What drives them? What do they hold dear? What are their values? When a manager knows their team members well, they can put their faith in them to get the job done to meet expectations. They'll know how to incentivize and engage them, and what challenges to place before them to help them grow. The net result is an engaged employee who is more than willing to put in extra effort and be trusted to do their best work for the company.

Not trusting employees can put a manager in a tough spot. After all, the manager needs the team to accomplish the work. However, it can be very prickly if the manager can't trust enough to create the supportive environment that encourages good work. In examining the problem, it could very well be the work of the manager that's causing the lack of trust. Here are some common triggers and what can be done about them:

- Unclear signals: It's hard for a manager to trust a team member if they're giving off signals the manager doesn't respond well to. For example, if a team member displays vulnerability and concern over certain aspects of the job, the manager may wonder about all the doubts and fears of the employees, and may not trust that the work will get done in the best fashion. Crossed signals are a barrier, but one that can be broken down with discussions and ongoing check-ins. Managers would be wise to really listen to what's being expressed, clarify any areas in question, and consider the employee's intentions and not the manager's gut reaction to what was stated.

- Different working styles: Generally speaking, there is more than one way to get things done. If a manager works one way and their team members work another, that doesn't mean the work isn't getting done well. It's easier for a manager to trust people who work in a similar fashion to theirs. However, not everyone does everything in exactly the same way. Businesses value diversity for all the innovation and creativity it can bring to a team. That means different styles and different ways of thinking. Managers must understand this is a good thing. Again, communication and transparency can help. If things must be done a certain way, managers need to state what they want and why, rather than drop hints and make vague statements that can be easily misinterpreted. Provide clear and specific instruction and feedback that will empower employees to make changes and deliver the desired results.

- Worrying the project is going off the rails: This is one of the problems Tom faced with his manager. While Tom had been checking in with the client and was assured expectations were being met, his manager's need to micromanage the project meant she unnecessarily called Tom in on his day off to do a bunch of work that was not really needed. The key is to make sure project milestones are clearly laid out and being measured and monitored regularly. Open communication is an indicator that things are going well; poor communication could be a warning sign that a lack of trust is warranted.[3]

- Talking too directly: Sometimes talking straight can be taken too far. In Simone's story, some of the things said to her by her boss were mean, even cruel. He was certainly transparent when he told her he didn't want her on his team. However, the way he delivered it left Simone with the sure knowledge she had to watch her back and couldn't trust her boss—which led him not to trust her. Being clear and straightforward is important, but this must be tempered with skill, tact, and good judgment.[4]

## Why should we care about trust?

In business, the difficult-to-measure factors, such as trust, might be considered unnecessary to doing business. However, trust has real economic factors tied to it. Trust affects two outcomes—speed and cost. If trust is high, things get done more quickly and at a lower cost. Conversely, if trust is low, it takes longer to get things done, and costs generally go up. Following is an example of this. I once worked for a boss who was the epitome of a micromanager. She questioned everything her team members did, including how we wrote emails. She insisted that every email had to be passed by her for approval before it was sent. This meant that any communications leaving her department took much longer to be sent, so the speed of work was slowed down greatly. In addition, costs increased due to time being wasted (and time is money) while the team had to wait for her to proof our work. We also had costs associated with the quality of work. Once we were finally able to execute, we had to rush things in order to complete them by deadlines. There was another cost as well—one that was actually pretty high. The lack of trust cost us dearly in terms of our working relationship. I was new on the job, so I was still trying to figure out how things worked. I would have loved to question why she hired me if she wasn't going to let me do the work, but I lacked the confidence to do that at this early stage with the company. Instead, I chafed against it and quietly fumed at my desk. Instead of being focused on my work, I was focused on how much I hated being under constant scrutiny. Eventually I drummed up the courage to question why my manager didn't trust my abilities to write an email. By this time, I was fed up with being treated, in my opinion, like a child, and was ready to quit. She was surprised to learn I felt that way, and immediately backed off. It turned out to be a good conversation that enabled me to resolve the issue, and as a result I went on to spend a number of years with that company, and truly loved my job, my coworkers and, yes, my manager. After that conversation, my manager trusted me to do great work, and in return I did quality work in an efficient and effective way. It's unfortunate the conversation had to be initiated by me, versus her putting some trust in the knowledge, skills, and abilities I came to the job with.

## Can trust be rebuilt once it's been broken?

Rebuilding trust once it's been broken is a very difficult thing. As mentioned above, trust is necessary for the establishment of safety and security, one of the most basic of human needs. When that is shattered, it may be impossible to put it back together again. However, it's also the case that we've all made mistakes at some point in our personal and professional lives. Because we've all made mistakes, the possibility of someone else understanding the situation and having empathy makes it possible (difficult, but possible) to regain trust.

When a manager has lost the trust of their employees, whether through poor judgment, reneging on promises, showing incompetence, or committing an honest mistake, the path to getting it back is through behaving with character and rebuilding credibility. Keep in mind, though, that the manager would need to change someone's feelings about them—no easy task.

If the breach of trust is considered to be a breach of character, the issue becomes quite a bit more complicated. However, it's possible to repair it by strengthening character through the following actions.[5]

- If trust has been broken because of lying, the first, and best, course of action is a *sincere* apology. Notice the emphasis on sincere. The perpetrator of the lie must take responsibility and apologize sincerely and humbly. There really is no other way to regain trust. Even if it's tough to admit a lie, admitting it will be a display of integrity. Making excuses or putting the blame on someone else will look like sloughing off the responsibility. To repair the rift, both an admission of guilt and a sincere apology are necessary.

- Remember, leaving out details of a story is also a lie–that is, a lie of omission. Employees will be suspicious of attempts to extricate oneself from the lie by claiming lack of knowledge or forgetting. As above, the best course of action is to admit the lie and apologize sincerely.

- If you've failed, admit it. Managers are human too, and that means they will fail from time to time. People are very tolerant with those who make mistakes, provided they are humble and set about rectifying what went wrong. If trust has been shaken by a displayed lack of competence, an apology is an important first step, but it's the actions taken to set things right that will help to re-establish trust. A sincere statement of what will be done and visible efforts to change will demonstrate commitment to making things better.

- There's a great deal of pressure put on managers all the time—goals, projections, tasks, and performance factors. If a manager has been caught over-promising and under-delivering, it's understandable their employees will find it hard to believe in them. To overcome this, managers should admit the past bad behaviour, and then set out a plan to achieve the goals laid out. Gradually, as goals are reached (as promised), employees will come to see the lesson has been learned and the behaviour has changed.

A trusting workplace is one that offers a culture in which employees and their managers can thrive. In this type of environment, everyone can feel free to be themselves and do their best work by taking risks, innovating, communicating, and succeeding.

## Why should managers work to create an environment of trust?

When leaders display character and competence, team members extend their trust back, rise to the occasion, strive to reach their potential, and make contributions that greatly benefit the organization. Not only that, this same extension of trust leads to a healthy and happy workplace culture in which people want to work, grow, and thrive. Trust brings out the best in people, and they want to live up to that trust. Extending trust to others brings happiness to relationships, results to work, and confidence to lives.[6]

Isn't that the type of environment everyone wants to work in?

**Some questions to ask about trust in a one on one:**

- What would you like me to be doing more of?
- What would you like me to do less of?
- What ideas do you have for improving things here?
- How can I help?
- What do you want to achieve?

# RESPECT Me

## 7 STEPS TO GET YOU ON THE PATH TO SOLVING ENGAGEMENT ISSUES IN YOUR WORKPLACE:

1. Develop a **RELATIONSHIP** with the people on your team.
2. Have **EMPATHY** for those you work with.
3. **SUPPORT** the members of your team.
4. **PROMOTE** the ideas of your team members and advocate for them.
5. **EMPOWER** them to be great on their own terms.
6. Have some **CONSIDERATION** for their feelings and for the work they've put in.
7. **TRUST** in them and be trustworthy yourself.

As you've seen from the stories and recommendations put forward in this book, it doesn't take fancy systems and tools to improve the situation with your team. You likely don't have to hire retention consultants and organizational psychologists to begin to fix what's not working so well. Of course, those things and people have their functions, and if things have really gone down a wrong path in your company, they may be necessary. For now though, start with the ideas presented in this book.

Begin with building relationships. There are absolutely no tools required to develop a relationship with your employees. All you need to do is create some time to *talk* with them. Block off time in your calendar for each of your team members. Start by giving them each an hour. Yes, I know this is a lot of time to take away from all the other demands that occupy us daily. However, this will be time well spent. These long meetings are required for you to start getting to know each other, and you may need more than a one-hour long meeting. After a couple of these longer meetings, you'll find your one on ones get shorter and you can likely catch up fully in half an hour. Remember, the goal of these meetings is to develop a relationship with the employee, so be sure to work on that first. Find out what's important to them on a personal basis, then proceed to task-related updates. Use the One on one Template I've provided to help you structure your meetings. (Find this template at www.cchangelearning.com/resources.) I hope you find it useful, and make it part of your routine. Alternatively, you might find you naturally fall into that cadence over time, and can work without the template. Whether you use the template or not, be sure to keep notes so you can follow through on any promises you made, or can follow up on progress during your next meeting. Following up means so much to your team members. It indicates you heard them and care about what they said.

Once you've gotten to know the people who work on your team, you'll understand what is important to them, what keeps them up at night, and what's happening in their lives. You'll also learn how progress is being made on important projects and tasks. Tracking this progress can help you solve small problems before they get big. If things start to head in the wrong direction, you'll be able to get back on the proper track quickly.

Most importantly, you're developing a relationship with your employee, such that you both can understand what is important to each other, what goals and objectives there are to pursue, and how they wish to grow and develop. By building a relationship, you're on your way to building trust.

If you've made the time to get to know your team members, you'll start appreciating them as individuals. They all have something to offer; what they offer can show up in different ways for each of them. By knowing them as people, you'll also learn what is truly important to them, and how what happens in their lives affects their work. Once you know them, it's highly likely you'll come to understand how they feel in given situations. Over time, you'll be able to put yourself in their shoes. If they become ill or need to tend to a family member, you'll truly understand what kind of support is needed. If they experience difficulty and/or pain in the workplace, you'll appreciate how it can affect their work. You'll come to treat them differently—with empathy.

When people are experiencing difficulties, they need a shoulder to lean on. If they know they can trust their manager, they'll appreciate experiencing the support and space they need to be able to focus on working through their challenges. It's possible they may recover faster, with a more positive outlook, and they'll certainly feel a much stronger sense of loyalty to their manager and the company. I speak from experience on this subject. I worked for a company that was in transition, and the outlook for my role wasn't so rosy. My manager faced the decision to let me go, but instead arranged for me to move to another team. My reporting relationship may have changed, but my position in the company was secured. As a result, my sense of loyalty to that company (and to my old *and* new managers) increased greatly. The two of them displayed empathy for me; they understood how important my job was to me and to the people I served in the company. In turn, I offered my best work and continued performing my role with gratitude.

That last story shows how having empathy for employees can inspire their loyalty. The same goes for support. When your people know you have their back, they'll respond by giving you their best effort. Team culture will blossom, and so will collaboration and innovation. When people feel supported, they are willing to try new things. Sure, they risk failure, but they can also innovate and create like never before when they're secure in the fact they're supported.

People have a need to feel valued at work and in life. When they feel they add value and are appreciated and supported at work, they will feel more secure and have a deeper level of trust in their managers, their company, and themselves. That level of trust gives employees the breathing space they need to be creative and confident, and as a result, do great work. When people feel supported and recognized, they also feel a desire to become even better at what they do.

When managers support their team members, this can have a ripple effect. Those who see how their coworkers are being supported and appreciated will learn to trust as well. They understand this is part of the team's culture and will in turn feel they can also expect and give support.

As a manager, you want your team members to do great work, grow, and develop. That's a good thing, after all. Why then, would you not help them to move into higher career levels? As Richard Branson said, "Train people well enough so they can leave. Treat them well enough so they don't want to." Promote their ideas and help them to move into higher positions. In your one on ones, have conversations about their developmental paths. If you promote their interests, they may move on from your team, but the company will be able to keep a valuable resource. If you don't promote their interests, they'll leave. Either way, you're losing that team member. However, in one of these scenarios the company benefits, and in the other, another company gets the benefit of that employee's knowledge and experience.

Promotion doesn't have to be just about moving people into new roles. It can also be about giving credit where credit is due. If your team members come up with innovative ideas, let higher-ups know where those ideas came from. If they create new processes and work flows that result in greater efficiencies, cost savings, or higher customer satisfaction, make sure they're acknowledged for the contribution and are made aware of how their work has positively impacted the department and the company. The benefit for the employee is credibility, visibility, and a higher profile within the company, and the benefit for you is loyalty and their best efforts. That's truly a win-win.

Great managers know the key to maximizing productivity is to empower their people to do great work. Empowered employees are able to think, take action, and make their own decisions, which results in greater productivity and successful project completion. Empowered employees understand what the team, department, and company need to achieve their goals, and they feel they can use their own knowledge, skills, abilities, and judgement to get there.

These people were hired into the role for a reason, so why not let them run with it and see what they can produce? If the manager has invested time in the relationship, they should know what work employees can take on, i.e., what will challenge them, and not drown them. They should also have open dialogue so important information is shared, like when a project is meeting its milestones … or when it's not. Why? Because empowered employees typically demonstrate greater loyalty and commitment to their companies. They feel engaged in and responsible for the work they do. As a result, they're more likely to follow proper procedures and produce higher-quality work. They're also more likely to provide excellent customer service (because they know they can!).

I mentioned engagement in the last paragraph. Engagement is directly impacted by the level of empowerment employees feel they have. Team members who feel empowered embrace change and opportunities for growth. They're not afraid of challenges, and will look for extra ways to contribute and collaborate. Why is this the case? Because they feel they have something to add and are in an environment that will embrace that way of thinking.

There's an old saying: "You catch more flies with honey than with vinegar." According to Wiktionary.com, this proverb means it's easier to persuade others with polite requests and a positive attitude than with rude demands and negativity. If you want your people to *want* to work with you, then you should treat them as human beings and as valued members of your team. When you run roughshod over their feelings, it's only natural they'd want to seek out a more understanding boss at another company or on a different team. Managers need to understand the ramifications of their words and actions on their team members.

Life at work is busy, and as a result, it's easy to forget about other people's circumstances and feelings. But caring is an important thing we all should be doing—regardless of our position. Respect and loyalty can't be bought.

When you are considerate of others, you're demonstrating loyalty and respect, and will receive them in turn.

Trust, or lack of it, can make or break an organization's culture. If it's important enough to break an organization, it can certainly cause irreparable damage to a team. Sadly, many employees are predisposed to not trust their managers. This could be due to past experiences with other managers, or having been downsized out of a previous job, and as a result they're preparing for the worst. Regardless of how it came about, a lack of trust will certainly colour an employee's relationship with their manager. However, earning the trust of employees is a crucial factor in being a great manager in a successful organization. It's also a crucial factor in retaining employees. Earning employees' trust is a daily practice, and must be part of all decisions a manager makes. As we learned from Stephen M.R. Covey, in his book *The Speed of Trust*, trust equals confidence, and distrust equals suspicion. If their team members trust them, managers will be rewarded with great work. If, on the other hand, their team members do not trust them, managers will be faced with suspicion and resistance to everything they ask their team to do.

Why is trust so important? Employees who don't trust their boss and/or company are far less likely to say good things about the company. This can affect future hiring and current retention. In addition, employees who are on the front lines will not be powerful advocates for the business if trust doesn't exist. Ensuring employees have trust in them and the company should be of great importance to managers. After all, it affects the employees, the work they do, and ultimately the customers.

# Wrapping It All Up

If you do a quick search of the internet, you'll find all kinds of tools and systems you can use to help you with engaging your employees. Some of them you may want to investigate are:

- Empathy Maps

- Individual Development Plans

- Personality Assessments

- Engagement Surveys

All of these tools have their places. However, the one tool you really **need** is the One on One Template. It's easily downloaded from my website www.cchangelearning.com. I'm a real believer in this tool, because I've personally witnessed and experienced the power of one on one conversations. As the manager, remember to take note of what is important to the employee and follow up in the next meeting. This will build the relationship, especially if you ask about something that's related to what *they* brought up, not you.

As you've seen throughout the book, effective working relationships between manager and team member don't happen magically. They take time, nurturing, and work, but they're always worth it.

When asked why they don't have these conversations, the number one reason cited by managers is lack of time. However, the short-term time savings of not having regular conversations is certainly offset by the time lost with projects that go off the rails, errors that are made, and replacing employees who have quit. Don't forget, time is money. Errors, loss of productivity, replacing employees, conflicts in the workplace, and misunderstandings all have costs attached to them. If you add up the costs in terms of time, effort, and money to overcome these negative situations, it's easy to see the benefit of the one on one.

I've always believed in the power of checking in with team members. I've spent my career in training, coaching, and mentoring others, and I can attest to the positive results these efforts can produce. So, yes, I'm biased. Having said that, in every one of the stories shared in this book, the people in question were seeking what consistent, regular, and frequent one on one conversations can deliver.

It's that attention and communication that occurs in these touch-base meetings that these former employees craved. Unfortunately, they didn't get it from their managers, so they ended up looking for it with another employer. All of that knowledge, all of those skills and abilities, walked out the door—at great cost to the employer, and great inconvenience to the manager. To compound the issues, these seven people are all now employed elsewhere (sometimes with the competition) and contributing their efforts to the benefit of the other companies. It seems such a shame, especially when this outcome could have been avoided with simple conversations.

It's not just these seven stories that demonstrate the importance of building a relationship with and having respect for employees. In pretty much every discussion I've had with people about the content of my book (and there have been many), I've heard stories of bad experiences people have had with their bosses. All of this may be anecdotal, but it's backed up by the data I've referenced throughout the book. Time after time we see that people break up with their managers because they didn't feel they were valued in the working relationship.

Much has been said and written over the last few years about the feeling of disconnection that has come about with the widespread use of technology taking the place of conversation. Office meetings were once places to collaborate and share ideas. Now attendees at these meetings have one eye on the speaker and the other on their computers—failing to pay proper attention to either. It pains me to see the way this has crept into manager-employee meetings. Technology has given us a perfect excuse to not have to speak to people face-to-face. Managers can simply ask their people to provide updates over email, or Slack instructions to them rather than having a conversation. This is fine in some cases, but it does nothing to help team members feel connected to the manager or the work.

Technology also causes disruption within meetings. As you've seen in this book, people are craving feedback, conversations, and connection with their manager. I've advocated for frequent and consistent conversations between manager and employee as a way to assert the importance of the employee to the workplace. If the manager spends more time looking at a computer monitor or phone during one on one meetings than they do looking at their team member (and believe me, this happens), it'll be abundantly clear to employees that whatever's going on on-screen is much more important than they are.

So, managers should bring their focus back to talking—really talking—to employees. Managers can solve so much by simply sharing their ideas, concerns, what's going well, and what could be improved. Employees can feel heard and understood, as well as appreciated. The One on one Template I've provided will help start these conversations. It can be used as a way to structure thoughts and ensure that important ideas are captured. It should also be used for follow-up, as it provides space to document what needs to be done, by when, and by whom. Once you start working with it, you'll realize the framework suggested is really very simple. You'll soon fall naturally into the cadence of discussing what's on the team member's mind, sharing what's on your mind, and discussing development opportunities. Things don't have to be complicated to work well. Sometimes it's the simplest things that work most elegantly.

If I've learned one thing from the Food Network, it's that simple dishes have to be executed perfectly. Not so with the one on one conversation. It's a simple concept, but the execution doesn't have to be flawless, just respected. Although I've provided some questions to get conversations started, you don't have to stick to these questions. What your team members want is the conversation itself. This is something that is simple and effective if you *just do it*. You'll get better at it over time—as will your team members. From time to time you may find yourself working off the template. That's not a problem. The big things to remember are:

- Allow time for your team member to speak what's on their mind
- Work in some time to talk about their development
- Take notes and follow up on the conversation
- Most importantly, honour the commitment to the one on one

Recently I've been challenged on this idea of having regular and frequent conversations with the people who report to me. The comments typically sound something like this: "Well, you don't have forty people reporting to you." That's true, I don't. But that doesn't make me waver from the one on one concept. It doesn't have to be dropped; it just needs to be tweaked. If you're in the position of having a large number of reports, you really, truly do have your work cut out for you to successfully manage such a large team. In my opinion, there's an organizational structure issue here that should really be dealt with. Layers should be put in place, at least incorporating team leaders, to help with the ongoing management and support of the team members. When the team is that large, how do companies prevent employees from feeling faceless and nameless? This puts a strain on the managers, but actions can be taken to try to make the best of a tough situation.

When managers have a very large team, they should do all they can to make contact with individual team members. It may seem there's not enough time in the day to have the quality conversations you'd like, but you can still make team members feel like you care about them individually. Try these ideas:

- Get up from your desk or out of your office and walk around the department. The business term is MBWA—Management By Walking Around. During your rounds, you can catch up on what's happening with people both on a business and personal basis.

## IT'S NOT THEM, IT'S YOU

Notice the pictures they have on their cubicle walls of their children and dogs. Ask them about the vacation souvenirs they have on their desks, and take a moment to just get to know them. Most importantly, by reaching out to them, you're building a relationship and demonstrating you're there when they need you.

- Empower your team members to make decisions for themselves. If you have a large team, you likely also have a large number of tasks. Respect the knowledge, skills, and abilities your reports bring to the table. Let them share some of the load. That'll free up time to have those one on one conversations everyone is seeking. At the same time, employees will be learning, growing, and feeling proud of the contributions they're making to the business.

- Use your subject matter experts to help build a supportive layer between you and your team. Have them coach and guide the others to develop their skills and increase their work scope. This will help keep your team learning new skills and becoming more well-rounded.

    You → Subject Matter Experts → Rest of the team

- Consider doing one on ones a little less frequently and doing group conversations a little more frequently. It's not ideal, but you're keeping the lines of communication open.

- Remember, communication isn't just about speaking – it's mostly about listening! Take any and all opportunities you can to listen to your team members.

- Doing the above things doesn't absolve you from having one on one conversations at all. Hold these focused and personal conversations as often as you can—at least once per month. If you have 40 reports, and you allocate ½ hour to each report once per month, that means you will devote 20 hours, over the course of the month, to one on one conversations. It sounds like a lot, but it's worth it to make time in your schedule.

For the rest of us who have a manageable number of reports, we must simply remember to schedule time for one on ones, honour that time commitment, make alternate plans if we have to cancel a one on one meeting, and ensure the meeting is about the employee, and not just about tasks that need to be done.

I came across a shocking statistic the other day (not sure why I found it so shocking, in light of what I've been writing about—but shocking nonetheless). Gallup Corporation, which I've referenced many times in this book, is the go-to resource for employee engagement information. They released this information:[1]

> When Gallup talked to exiting workers, they found two fascinating bits of information: First, more than half (52%) of them said their manager or organization could have done something to keep them from leaving. Second, 51% said that in the three months before their departure, neither their manager nor any other company leader had spoken with them about their job satisfaction or their future.

It's the second of those statistics that I find so sad. I am certain—regardless of team size, *certain*—that any manager can find time in a three-month span to talk to their reports. Imagine the sense of isolation and neglect employees feel when no one in the company checks in on them for months! I knew this kind of thing happened, and this is what Rosalie experienced from her boss. I guess I just didn't realize how pervasive it is. A simple conversation may have had the power to keep these contributing employees with their companies. To me, there really is no excuse.

What do the engagement experts suggest to overcome this problem?

At the end of its report, Gallup suggested, "Train your managers to have frequent, meaningful conversations with employees about what really matters to them. What's frustrating them? What are their dreams? Where do they want to go?"

You now have this powerful management tool—the One on One Template. Go and use it with your teams. And when you have conversations with your people, document what they tell you on the template for follow-up. Remember what Gallup found in their research—your reports want you to have frequent, meaningful conversations with them.

Recently, I had a conversation with a new manager. She was speaking to me about what she has learned from me and other sources in the way of leadership lessons. We spoke of the importance of conversation and follow-up, of supporting and trusting your reports, and of developing a relationship with them. We spoke about how humanity seems to be missing from so many workplaces, and how people are so focused on the tasks they have to complete that they forget about the people who are working very hard to get them done.

I feel her closing thoughts from our conversation are the best way to close this book. She told me what she thought people really need from their bosses is to be treated like humans … and with respect. I couldn't agree more.

# Acknowledgements and Gratitude

This passion project of mine would not have happened without those who have shared their stories. I've spoken to countless people who have had bad experiences with their managers. However, it is these seven brave people who came forward to share their stories with the world, in the hope they will make a difference. I am so grateful to each of you—Rosalie, Emily, Simone, Percy, Elton, Caitlin, and Tom. You know who you are.

To the Brilliance Brunch Bunch—you have all encouraged me. Through the talking, laughing, and hugging, I have felt buoyed up even when things got bogged down. Teresa Duke, Lorie Corcuera, Fabiana Gennari, and Lisa Martin, you are such important people not only to this project, but to my life. Thank you for your friendship.

To the Awesome Women crew—how fortunate I am to have you in my life! Glorie Averbach, Betty Hasker, Nuria Sefchovich, and Efe Fruci, you are all inspirations and I can't thank you enough for pulling me up when I started to sink. Your enthusiastic words ring in my heart!

Kirsten Anderson—you are an amazing human being. I am so glad I reached out to you about bringing this content to life in workshops. We've brought the message to a lot of people by now, and I bet we've made some changes to workplaces out there. Thank you for your creativity and your sense of fun. Most of all, thank you for seeing my vision and helping me make it happen.

Stephanie Redivo—thank you for championing my efforts and for taking a chance on me when you heard that crazy workshop concept that apparently really works well! You've been a sounding board and an advice giver, and I am so very grateful for it.

To Melody Biringer, Gina Fresquez, Nadine Stille, elan Bailey, and all my other WIT Regatta friends—thank you for giving me a platform on which to speak and through which to realize my potential. I have become a much more confident person as a result of meeting all of you, and I am so happy about it. I'm not sure I would have had the courage to write this book had I not experienced the Regatta and your support.

Alison Caldwell-Johnson—thank you for coaching me and making me set free what I knew in my heart to be right. Because of you, I was able to believe I deserve this and that I really can (and should) make this happen. Also, thank you for helping with the title. When you serendipitously stated what I already thought could be the title, I knew I had something.

Catherine Corley—how kind of you to offer to edit this first-timer's book. I hope it hasn't been too arduous for you. Fingers crossed!

To my parents—thank you for being proud of me. I know this venture has been a little hard for you to understand, since it seemed to have come out of left field. But you are right there with me. For that I am truly grateful.

To Chris Walton and Laurie Stewart—it will likely come as a relief to you that this book is finally done! You've heard me talk on and on about it for so long. Well, here it is! Thanks for being there for me all along the way.

To Abby Lawson and Justin Ledger—you were two of the first people to hear this idea that day in Dubai. When I had my doubts, the two of you countered them with encouragement. Thanks so much!

Finally, to my husband Robin, and my daughter Natasha—you have believed in me every single step of the way. You are the first people I turned to when things got rough, and you are the first people I turned to in celebration when I finished writing. I am so very fortunate to have you both in my corner. So very much love!

# Sources

## LET'S START WITH THE STORIES

1.  Gallup, "State of the American Manager Report," 2018.

2.  Valerie Bolden-Barrett, *Study: Many plan to job hunt after less than a year on the job*, (HR Dive, Dec. 2018).

3.  *Over Eighty Percent of Full-time Workers are Actively Seeking or Passively Open to New Job Opportunities* (Ajilon, July 2018).

4.  Udemy In Depth: *2018 "Employee Experience Report,"* (Udemy, 2018).

## ROSALIE

1.  Gallup, "State of the American Manager Report," 2018.

## EMILY

1.  Richard Boyatzis and Annie McKee, *Resonant Leadership: Renewing Yourself and Connecting with Others Through Mindfulness, Hope, and Compassion* (Boston: Harvard Business School Press, 2005).

2.  Monica C. Worline and Jane E. Dutton, *Awakening Compassion at Work* (Oakland: Berrett-Koehler Publishers, 2017) 166.

3.  Monica C. Worline and Jane E. Dutton, *Awakening Compassion at Work* (Oakland: Berrett-Koehler Publishers, 2017) 120.

## CAITLIN

1.  Michael Booz, LinkedIn Talent Blog, "These 3 Industries Have the Highest Talent Turnover Rates" (LinkedIn March 15, 2018).

## TOM

1.  Stephen M.R. Covey, *The Speed of Trust* (New York: Free Press, 2006).

2.  Stephen M.R. Covey, *The Speed of Trust* (New York: Free Press, 2006) 29.

## INFOGRAPHIC

1.  Gallup "State of the American Manager Report," 2018.

## RELATIONSHIPS

1.  Rob Goffee and Gareth Jones, *Why Should Anyone Be Led by You?* (Boston: Harvard Business School Press, 2015).

2.  Simon Sinek, *Start with Why* (New York: Penguin Group, 2009) 55.

3.  Gallup "State of the American Manager Report," 2018.

4.  Paul Petrone, "How to Calculate the Cost of Employee Disengagement," LinkedIn 2017.

5.  Sarah Brown, Daniel Gray, Jolian McHardy, Karl Taylor, "Employee Trust and Workplace Performance," *Journal of Economic Behaviour and Organization*, (May 2015).

6.  Daniel Sgroi, "Happiness and Productivity: Understanding the Happy-Productive Worker," (Social Market Foundation, Global Perspectives Series: Paper 4). (December 10, 2015)

7. Officevibe, "The Before, During & After Guide for the Perfect One on one," Officevibe (January 26, 2018)

8. Elizabeth Grace Saunders, "Cancelling One on one Meetings Destroys Your Productivity," *Harvard Business Review*, (March 9, 2015).

## EMPATHY

1. Rise Staff, "Personal and Sick Leave: Recommendations and Requirements," (Risepeople.com blog, April 2018).

2. Kim Cameron, Carlos Mora, Trevor Leutscher, and Margaret Calarco, "Effects of Positive Practices on Organizational Effectiveness," *Journal of Applied Behavioral Science* 47, no. 3 (January 26, 2011).

3. Monica C. Worline and Jane E. Dutton, *Awakening Compassion at Work* (Oakland, CA: Berrett-Kohler, 2017).

4. James Burns, *Leadership* (New York: Harper & Row 1978).

5. Zameena Mejia, "Marc Benioff and Jeff Weiner are Among America's 10 Most-Liked CEOs of 2018," (CNBC.com, June 20, 2018).

6. Jeff Weiner, "Managing Compassionately," (LinkedIn Pulse, Oct. 14, 2012).

## SUPPORT

1. Simon Sinek, *Start with Why* (Penguin Press, New York, NY, 2009).

2. Tony Schwartz and Christine Porath, "The Power of Meeting Your Employees' Needs," (HBR.org, June 30, 2014).

3. Christine L. Porath and Amir Erez, "Overlooked but Not Untouched: How Rudeness Reduces Onlookers' Performance on

Routine and Creative Tasks," *Organizational and Human Decision Processes,* Vol. 109, Issue 1, (May 2009).

4. Drew Hansen, "7 Steps to Increase Self-Awareness and Catapult your Career," (Forbes.com, Jan. 24, 2012).

5. Sleep Country Canada ad, (Youtube.com, 2018) https://youtu.be/GtCW8tYafJE.

6. Patrick Hyland, "If You Don't Know How to Manage Yourself, You Shouldn't Be Managing Others," (Mercer Sirota blog, Aug. 16, 2017).

7. AMA Staff, "Get the Most from Your People: Give 'Em What They Want," *American Management Association* (January 24, 2019).

8. Stephen M.R. Covey, *The Speed of Trust* (New York: Free Press, 2006) 140.

9. Amy Gallo, "How to Manage Someone You Don't Like," *Harvard Business Review,* (August 29, 2013).

10. Elizabeth from the Social Workplace, "Employee Engagement: What Employees Need and What Managers Can Do," (The Social Workplace blog, Nov. 23, 2011).

## PROMOTION

1. Gallup, "How Millennials Want to Work and Live," (2018).

2. Brandon Rigoni and Bailey Nelson, "When Making Career Moves, Americans Switch Companies," *Business Journal,* (Oct. 22, 2015).

3. Victor Lipman, "Why Employee Development is Important, Neglected and Can Cost You Talent," *Forbes,* (Jan. 29, 2013).

## EMPOWERMENT

1. Quote: Charles-Guillaume Etienne.

2. Jeff Toister, "Five Reasons Why Managers Don't Empower Employees," *Toister Performance Solutions*, (Mar. 10, 2015).

3. A.D. Amar, Carsten Hentrich, Vlatka Hlupic, "To Be a Better Leader, Give Up Authority," *Harvard Business Review*, (Dec. 2009).

4. LaHuann Moore, "5 Reasons Why You Should Empower Your Workers," (MGMT Blog, *Institute of Certified Professional Managers*, November 16, 2018).

5. Kevin Daum, "8 Tips for Empowering Employees," (*Inc.* Sept. 30, 2013).

6. Ken Blanchard and Spencer Johnson, *The New One Minute Manager* (New York: HarperCollins, 2015).

## CONSIDERATION

1. Stephen M.R. Covey, *The Speed of Trust* (New York: Free Press, 2006) 145.

2. Stephen R. Covey, *The Seven Habits of Highly Effective People* (New York: Free Press, 2004) 239.

3. Knowledge at Wharton, "Declining Employee Loyalty: A Casualty of the New Work Place," (Pennsylvania: Wharton University, 2012).

4. Bureau of Labor Statistics, "Employee Tenure in 2018," (US Department of Labour, Sept. 20, 2018).

## TRUST

1. Stephen M.R. Covey, *The Speed of Trust* (New York: Free Press, 2006) 5.

2. Stephen M.R. Covey, *The Speed of Trust* (New York: Free Press, 2006) 30.

3. Wanda T. Wallace and David Creelman, "What to Do When You Don't Trust Your Team," *Harvard Business Review*, (Sept. 30, 2015).

4. Stephen M.R. Covey, *The Speed of Trust* (New York: Free Press, 2006) 140.

5. Susan M. Heathfield, "Ways to Rebuild Trust at Work," *The Balance Careers*, (Feb. 10, 2019).

6. Stephen M.R. Covey, *The Speed of Trust* (New York: Free Press, 2006) 322.

## WRAPPING IT ALL UP

1. Bruce Anderson, "Gallup Suggests That Employee Turnover in U.S. Business Is a $1 Trillion Problem—With a Simple Fix" (*LinkedIn Talent*, April 25, 2019).

# About the Author

Laura Sukorokoff has always had a passion for the employee experience. She has built a career in learning and organizational development and seeks to make work a great place to be. Laura is a highly regarded speaker and subject matter expert in the area of engagement and retention. She works with leaders, entrepreneurs, managers, coaches, and professionals in all facets of business.

While she actually dislikes the term soft skills (she far prefers calling them "Power Skills!" instead), Laura loves to coach and support others in their learning and adoption of these highly valued professional skills. She knows these actually-very-hard-to-learn skills are key to success in management, business, and life.

Laura brings a fresh way of thinking to employee engagement and retention. She firmly believes managers hold the key to making workplaces more human and her company, C-Change Learning and Development, provides those managers with the knowledge and support they need to get that done.

When not at work, Laura enjoys exploring new places and meeting new people around the world, hanging out with her husband and daughter in their Vancouver home, or exploring the woods with her two dogs, Doug and Murray.

Photo credit: Suzanne Rushton Photography

Printed in Canada